WOMEN'S INSTITUTE
COMPLETE CHRISTMAS

WOMEN'S INSTITUTE

COMPLETE CHRISTMAS

SIAN COOK ✳ MARGARET WILLIAMS ✳ ANNE GRIFFITHS

TED SMART

First published in Great Britain by Simon & Schuster UK Ltd. 2004
A Viacom Company

This edition produced for The Book People Ltd,
Hall Wood Avenue, Haydock, St Helens WA11 90L

ISBN 0 74325 937 8

Simon & Schuster UK Ltd
Africa House
64–78 Kingsway
London
WC2B 6AH

The right of Sian Cook, Margaret Williams and Anne Griffiths to be identified as the
Authors of this Work has been asserted by them in accordance with sections 77 and
78 of the Copyright, Design and Patents Act, 1988.

1 3 5 7 9 10 8 6 4 2

Text design: Jane Humphrey
Typesetting: Stylize Digital Artwork Ltd
Food photography: Juliet Piddington
Home economist: kathryn Hawkins
Stylist for food photography: Helen Trent
Index by Anne Doggett
Photograph on page 38 by Steve Baxter
Printed and bound in China

ACKNOWLEDGEMENTS

Sian Cook

There are so many people I would like to thank. As ever, I would like to thank my family for all their help, encouragement and support. Their patience in putting up with endless 'testers' has really been appreciated. Unfortunately, Amy had to be excluded from tasting most of the dishes as she is on a special diet and can only eat puréed food – Terry and Holly probably thought she was the lucky one! Once again, my husband, Terry, has been invaluable with his IT skills, as has Holly, who is much better than her mother!

I would also like to thank my friends for being willing guinea pigs and for their constructive comments. I was popular with them for the samples they were given!

Finally, I would like to thank my local Tesco store in Newbury for donating some food for recipe tasting. It was greatly appreciated.

Margaret Williams

To my husband, Michael, for all his help and support, particularly with typing up the recipes onto the computer.

To family and friends who have sampled the recipes and given valuable feedback.

To Billingtons for supplying us with quantities of their wonderful sugars. Their generosity was much appreciated.

Anne Griffiths

I would like to thank my husband Steve for his support and help during this project, for listening to some of my more 'imaginative' ideas and putting up with the kitchen being in uproar and used as a general workshop!

To my dear friends Frances and Jim for their appreciation of the prototype designs at one rather damp New Year's Eve dinner party, and to everyone else who has given help and suggestions freely. You are all much appreciated.

Olive Oil with Chilli + Garlic

8   INSPIRATIONS FOR CHRISTMAS

10   CHRISTMAS ESSENTIALS

38   DECEMBER 23rd AND 24th

58   CHRISTMAS DAY

82   CHRISTMAS DAY TIMETABLE

84   VEGETARIAN CHRISTMAS

102   CHEAT'S CHRISTMAS

120   CHRISTMAS BRUNCHES

134   CHRISTMAS LEFTOVERS

154   PARTIES AND CELEBRATIONS

192   CHRISTMAS DRINKS

202   MENU PLANNERS

205   RECIPE INDEX

208   CRAFT INDEX

Contents

Inspirations for Christmas

Christmas is the time of year for enjoying the company of family and friends, but this can be lost in the frantic lead up to the big day. I'm sure we've all said it many times: "all this fuss over one day" but it's definitely worth the effort. It can be such a bright and happy time, with parties and celebrations and a chance to be hospitable. We can indulge in delicious meals without thinking about calories and have a perfect excuse to decorate our homes, both inside and out, with festive decorations that would be considered over the top at any other time. It's also a great opportunity to get out the best china and tableware to make all the meals extra special.

Christmas can be a little daunting when you think about all the work involved in making it a a huge success. If you are looking for inspiration and guidance to make sure that everyone has a wonderful time – whether it's making gifts, decorations, centre-pieces for the table and, of course, delicious food and drink – and you want instructions and recipes that are foolproof and easy to follow, then this book is for you!

Supermarkets are full of food that is ready to eat or heat in the oven. It looks extremely appetizing so it's very tempting to fill up your trolley with convenience foods but, apart from the cost of buying only convenience food, the quality rarely matches up to that of its homemade equivalent. We're all for a bit of cheating now and again but the appreciative comments from your family and friends when you serve up delicious homemade meals make it well worth the effort.

In this book there are recipes for all occasions over the festive period, some traditional and some taking into account current tastes and trends. Many of them have been prepared with busy lifestyles in mind. Quite a few recipes have tips to help make them a success – we always find tips invaluable and have learnt so much over the years simply by applying them.

When we were younger we couldn't understand why our parents made such a fuss about who they invited for Christmas, when to throw a party and planning the food for these festive occasions. We can understand it now and are sure that our families think much the same about us! When December approaches, we start making endless lists – Christmas presents to get and make, menus for different occasions, together with several shopping lists and dates for inviting friends over. It must sound so boring but making lists is the only way we can cope and know that we won't forget anything! We've also come to the conclusion that planning is the key to enjoying this time of year. The more we can prepare in advance, the more likely it is that we'll be able to enjoy the festivities.

We've had enormous fun writing this book – we hope you will have as much fun using it each Christmas.

SÎAN AND MARGARET

Christmas
Essentials

One of the reasons we all love Christmas is because it is steeped in tradition. Most families have their own traditions, which are often handed down from generation to generation – most family Christmases recall those of our childhood.

It is unrealistic to make everything for the festive period. We hope that the following recipes will inspire you to make some. The beauty of all of them is that they can be made in advance and, in the case of some of them, such as Christmas cake and pudding, actually benefit from being made well ahead, when you have some spare time

We have included a number of festive cakes and hopefully there is one to suit your taste and time – you may want to make them all! Likewise with Christmas Puddings – the Fruity one is light and quick to cook in the microwave, while Gran's is prepared in the traditional way. In addition to the other Christmas 'must-haves', such as mince pies and rum sauce, there are recipes for a short-cut Stollen and Millionaire Shortbread Biscuits. We hope there is something for everyone.

Jewelled Christmas Cake *(page 15)*

CHRISTMAS CAKE

I was given this recipe about 18 years ago and have made it each year since. I have never had a disappointing result – it always produces a delicious, moist cake with an abundance of flavour. It is important to take the time to prepare the tin as this ensures a moist cake. Holly's favourite colours are lilac and silver and so the decoration incorporates these as they look effective set against the white icing. Preparation time: 40 minutes Soaking + cooling: 12 hours Cooking time: 8 hours

brown paper of double thickness
350 g (12 oz) each of currants and
    sultanas
225 g (8 oz) raisins
6 tablespoons brandy
300 g (10 oz) butter, softened
300 g (10 oz) soft brown sugar
6 large eggs, lightly beaten
1 tablespoon treacle
250 g (9 oz) plain flour
grated rind of 1 orange
115 g (4 oz) mixed peel
175 g (6 oz) glacé cherries, halved
50 g (2 oz) whole almonds
a pinch of salt
½ teaspoon each of ground
    cinnamon and mixed spice
50 g (2 oz) ground almonds
175 g (6 oz) apricot jam

1 Place the currants, sultanas and raisins in a large bowl, pour over half the brandy and stir with a spoon to ensure that all the fruit is coated in the brandy. Cover with cling film and leave to soak for at least 12 hours or overnight.

2 Pre-heat the oven to Gas Mark ¼/electric oven 110°C/fan oven 90°C.

3 Prepare the cake tin – you will need one that is 20 cm (8 inches) and has a depth of at least 9 cm (3½ inches) – see page 15, Jewelled Christmas Cake. In addition to this you will need to cut a 25 cm (10 inch) circle of brown paper of double thickness (I sometimes use old A4 envelopes) to go on top.

4 Place the butter and sugar in a very large mixing bowl and whisk until it is light and fluffy.

5 Add the eggs gradually, whisking well between each addition.

6 Add the treacle with a little of the flour and whisk until it is incorporated. Add the orange rind, mixed peel, cherries, almonds and the soaked fruit. Sift the remaining flour with the salt and spices and then fold into the mixture. Finally, mix in the ground almonds and the remaining brandy.

7 Spoon the mixture into the prepared tin, level the surface and then, using the back of a tablespoon, make a dip in the centre – this will ensure that the cake has a flat surface when cooked.

8 Wrap the brown paper around the tin and secure with string or sticky tape. Place the brown paper circle on top and secure it to the band with sticky tape.

9 Bake in the oven for 8 hours – the cake is ready when a skewer inserted in the middle comes out clean. Leave to cool in the tin for a short while and then remove the cake and cool it on a wire rack.

10 To make the apricot glaze, put the jam into a saucepan with 2 tablespoons of water and heat gently to melt the jam. Stir from time to time. Rub the jam mixture through a sieve into a clean saucepan, bring back to the boil and simmer for a minute. Allow to cool before brushing evenly all over the cake.

 Freezing not recommended

SCC

MARZIPAN

Ready-made marzipan is available in supermarkets. However, I would urge you to make your own as it takes very little time and is far superior. Make sure that you store the Christmas cake uncovered, at room temperature for at least a day before icing it. You can store the marzipan for up to 2 days.

Makes 900 g (2 lb) Preparation time: 10 minutes + 2 days storing + 20 minutes icing cake

225 g (8 oz) caster sugar
225 g (8 oz) icing sugar, sifted,
   plus extra for dusting
225 g (8 oz) ground almonds
2 teaspoons lemon juice
4 egg yolks, lightly beaten

1 Place the sugars and ground almonds in a bowl. Make a well in the middle and add the lemon juice and egg yolks. Bring the mixture together to form a dough. Wrap it in cling film or foil and store for up to two days before using.

To ice the Christmas cake (opposite)
2 Place almost half the marzipan on a work surface dusted with icing sugar and roll out to a circle which is 22.5 cm (9 inches) in size. Lift the marzipan circle onto the cake. Trim off any excess marzipan and smooth the edges with a palette knife.

3 Cut two pieces of string, one the same height as the cake and the other the complete circumference. Roll out the rest of the marzipan and, using the string to help you, cut a strip to the height and circumference of the cake – a long ruler will help you with straight lines. Roll up the piece loosely and place one end on the side of the cake and unroll with care, pressing the marzipan to the cake as you go and making sure that it touches the cake board all the way around.

4 Using a palette knife, smooth all the joins so that there are no obvious seams.

 Freezing not recommended

Tip: When bringing the marzipan together, it is easier to do so by placing it in a plastic bag and rolling it into a ball.

N.B. This recipe contains raw eggs – pregnant women, the elderly, babies and toddlers should avoid eating raw eggs.

SCC

ROYAL ICING

You can store this icing in an airtight container in a cool place for a couple of days but you will need to stir it before use and possibly add a little extra sifted icing sugar. Adding glycerine helps to soften the icing and makes it easier to cut. **Makes 675 g (1½ lb)** Preparation time: 15 minutes + icing time + 24 hours drying time

3 egg whites
675 g (1½ lb) icing sugar, sifted
3 teaspoons lemon juice, strained
1½ teaspoons glycerine
To decorate
silver balls
small piece of ready-made fondant
  icing
purple food colouring
1.5 m (5 feet) of lilac and silver
  snowflake ribbon, or one of
  your choice

1 Put the egg whites in a large mixing bowl and whisk until they are frothy. Using a wooden spoon, gradually beat in half the icing sugar (don't be tempted to use an electric whisk as it will incorporate too much air and create bubbles).
2 Add the lemon juice, glycerine and half the remaining icing sugar. Beat well until the icing is smooth. Gradually beat in the remaining icing sugar, a little at a time until the icing stands in soft peaks.

3 Put the icing in a bowl and cover with cling film. Leave for an hour to allow any bubbles to come to the surface and burst.
4 Spoon the icing onto the top of the cake and, using a palette knife, spread it evenly over the top and sides of the cake until there is no marzipan visible. It may help to dip the knife occasionally into a mug of hot water. Smooth the sides so that they are as even as possible Bring the icing on the top of the cake up to peaks using the tip of the knife. Place a silver ball on top of each of the peaks.
5 Use a tiny amount of the colouring to colour the fondant icing lilac. Roll out fairly thinly and cut out small star shapes. Place these on top of the cake in between the silver balls.
6 Leave the iced cake to dry, uncovered, for 24 hours. Use enough of the ribbon to wrap around the cake and secure with a couple of sewing pins. Tie the remaining piece of ribbon into a bow and position where the sewing pins are, again using pins, which you can then conceal.

 *Freezing not recommended*

N.B. This recipe contains raw eggs – pregnant women, the elderly, and babies and toddlers should avoid eating raw eggs.

SCC

JEWELLED CHRISTMAS CAKE

This cake, with its decorative fruit topping, glistens like the jewels in a crown and definitely deserves centre stage on the Christmas tea table. Serve with a glass of tawny port and a wedge of Wensleydale cheese. **Serves 18** Preparation time: overnight soaking + 30 minutes Cooking time: 2–2¼ hours

175 g (6 oz) glazed pineapple, chopped

175 g (6 oz) mixed cherries (red, green and yellow), halved

125 g (4½ oz) dried apricots, chopped

50 g (2 oz) candied peel or citron peel, chopped by hand

125 g (4½ oz) sultanas

25 g (1 oz) crystallised ginger, chopped

6 tablespoons Bacardi rum

225 g (8 oz) butter

225 g (8 oz) unrefined light caster sugar

4 eggs, beaten

225 g (8 oz) self-raising flour

75 g (2¾ oz) Brazil nuts, chopped

100 g (3½ oz) ground almonds

To decorate

apricot jam

nuts, glacé and dried fruits, e.g. glacé cherries, stem ginger, candied citrus peel

ribbon to tie around the cake

1 Soak all the fruit, along with the ginger, in rum overnight.

2 Grease and line a 20 cm (8 inch) round or an 18 cm (7 inch) square cake tin. (For method see below).

3 Cream the butter and sugar together until light and fluffy.

4 Add the eggs gradually, beating well, after each addition.

5 Add the flour and fold in carefully.

6 Stir in the soaked fruit with the Brazil nuts and ground almonds.

7 Transfer the cake mixture to the prepared tin, making sure that it is pushed well into the corners and edges, then level the surface. Dip a tablespoon in boiling water, then rub the back of the spoon over the cake surface to make it smooth.

8 Bake for 2–2¼ hours in the oven at Gas Mark 2/electric oven 150°C/fan oven 130°C until it is golden brown and firm to the touch. Insert a skewer into the centre and if it comes out clean, the cake is cooked.

9 Remove the cake from the oven and leave to cool in the tin.

10 When completely cold, remove from the cake from the tin. Peel off the baking parchment and rewrap the cake in paper and foil or store in an airtight tin. The Christmas cake can be left to mature for up to 4 weeks before decorating.

Lining the cake tin

One of the keys to success when baking fruit cakes is the preparation of the tin before you start mixing the ingredients. Because of the length of cooking time, you need to use two sheets of greaseproof paper or baking parchment inside the tin.

1 Lightly oil the inside of the tin.

2 Cut out a strip of paper about 2.5 cm (1 inch) longer than the outside of the tin and 5 cm (2 inches) wider. (measure using a piece of string),

3 Fold in about 2 cm (¾ inch) along the long edge of the strip. Then make diagonal cuts along the folded edge at 2.5 cm (1 inch) intervals.

4 Fit the long strip of paper inside the tin with the folded edge sitting flat on the base. If you have a square tin fit the paper tightly into the corners.

5 Place the tin on two sheets of greaseproof paper or baking parchment and draw around the base of the tin. Cut two pieces of paper to fit snugly into the base of the tin.

6 Before baking, tie some thick brown paper or newspaper, which comes above the tin by about 10 cm (4 inches), around the edge of the tin.

To decorate

1 Brush the top of the cake with sieved apricot jam. Arrange your choice of fruit on the top in an attractive pattern and use more apricot jam to glaze the top of the fruit.

2 Tie a ribbon around the middle of the cake that complements the colour of the fruit.

 Freezing not recommended

Tip: To prevent your cake from sinking, never open the oven door until at least half the cooking time has elapsed.

MEW

CHRISTMAS SNOWFLAKES

Lacy snowflakes can be made in a variety of sizes and used to decorate presents and cards or they can be hung from a mantelpiece or Christmas tree. Made from shiny paper, they can be stuck on to decorate plain wrapping paper or use tiny ones as gift tags or to hang on a mobile. You could use them as templates and spray them with either gold paint to decorate paper or straight on to window panes with fake snow. The beauty of snowflakes is that no two will be exactly the same, as in nature!

You will need:
- paper; shiny is pretty
- small, pointed scissors
- gold paint (optional) or fake snow

1 To make the snowflake, cut a square of paper to the size you want the finished snowflake.
2 Fold the paper in half diagonally and then fold twice more. Make the creases when you are happy with the folds.
3 Using small pointed scissors, cut off the corners and then cut out zigzags, snipping other smaller bits out on either side. You can also snip off the point. Be sure to leave some uncut pieces along the folds or the snowflake will fall apart.
4 When you have your snowflake design, gently unfold the paper and iron flat if necessary.

BEADED WIRE STARS

The aim of this project is to make stars approximately 6 cm (2½ inches) in diameter, which can be hung from a Christmas tree or mantelpiece, or incorporated into a flower arrangement, table decoration or wreath.

There is a huge range of wires in a variety of colours and gauges available in craft shops these days and they can be bought in small skeins which should make 2 or 3 stars.

You will need:
- wire that is fairly thick but still fine enough to pass through the holes in your beads.
- 2 packets of beads (seed beads, bugles or a mixture of both)
- Thread or ribbon for hanging

1 To make a star, cut a piece of wire about 38 cm (15 inches) long and, using the wire like a needle, thread on enough beads to cover the wire, leaving a couple of inches uncovered.
2 Making sure you have no beads on the first 4 cm (1½ inches) of wire, bend it over to stop the beads slipping off. Do the same on the other end, leaving a little more wire uncovered. Now bend the middle section, with all the beads on, into an even zigzag with 5 more points at the bottom and 6 points at the top.
3 To complete the star, twist the longer end of uncovered wire round the shorter one and make a loop for hanging. Slip a piece of thread or ribbon through the loop if necessary. If your star is a little unstable, wind some more wire across the centre section to make it sturdier.

AG

CHOCOLATE CHRISTMAS CAKE

This moist fruit cake will be popular with chocoholics – the addition of the chocolate doesn't dominate but it gives the cake a lovely rich flavour. You can decorate it as you would a traditional Christmas cake or simply serve it as it is but decorate it with a big seasonal ribbon. Preparation time: 20 minutes + cooling Cooking time: 1¾–2 hours

150 g (5 oz) soft margarine

150 g (5 oz) light muscovado sugar

2 eggs, lightly beaten

185 g (6½ oz) self-raising flour

40 g (1½ oz) cocoa powder

400 g jar of luxury mincemeat

80 g (3 oz) each of sultanas and raisins

50 g (2 oz) blanched almonds, chopped

100 g packet of white chocolate chips

1 Pre-heat the oven to Gas Mark 3/electric 160ºC/fan oven 140ºC. Line a 20 cm (8 inch) cake tin following the instructions on page 16, Jewelled Christmas Cake .

2 Place all the ingredients in a large mixing bowl and beat together for a minute or two until all the ingredients are thoroughly mixed.

3 Spoon into the prepared tin and bake in the oven for 1¾–2 hours until a skewer inserted into the centre comes out clean. You will probably need to cover the cake with foil towards the end of cooking to prevent the top from browning too much.

4 Leave the cake to cool in the tin for a few minutes before turning out onto a wire rack to cool completely.

 Freezing not recommended

SCC

FRUITY CHRISTMAS PUDDING

This pudding makes a light finish to the Christmas meal and can be made on the day in a microwave oven. It also has the advantage of not taking up a ring on the hob while preparing the rest of the Christmas lunch.

Serves 8–10 Preparation time: 25 minutes + overnight soaking + 5 minutes standing Cooking time: 20 minutes

75 g (2$\frac{3}{4}$ oz) raisins

75 g (2$\frac{3}{4}$ oz) sultanas

50 g (2 oz) chopped glacé pineapple

50 g (2 oz) cherries, cut into quarters

50 g (2 oz) crystallised ginger peel, chopped

4 tablespoons brandy

50 g (2 oz) ground almonds

50 g (2 oz) fresh breadcrumbs

grated rind and juice of 1 orange

50 g (2 oz) Brazil nuts, chopped

50 g (2 oz) 2 cooking apples peeled and cored, grated

50 g (2 oz) carrot, grated

125 g (4$\frac{1}{2}$ oz) butter

125 g (4$\frac{1}{2}$ oz) dark muscovado sugar

2 eggs, beaten

125 g (4$\frac{1}{2}$ oz) wholemeal self-raising flour

$\frac{1}{2}$ teaspoon ginger

$\frac{1}{2}$ teaspoon cinnamon

2 tablespoons milk

1 tablespoon black treacle

To serve

2 tablespoons brandy

Brandy Butter (see p 22)

1 In bowl one: put the first six ingredients and mix together. Soak overnight, covered, in a cool place.

2 In bowl two: mix together the next six ingredients. Combine the contents of bowls one and two.

3 In a mixing bowl cream together the butter and sugar until light and fluffy. Add the beaten egg a little at a time. Do not worry if the mixture curdles, just add a tablespoon of the flour and stir in. Add the remaining flour and spices and combine with the creamed mixture. Stir in the contents of bowls one and two and mix well. Add 2 tablespoons of milk. For microwaving, the consistency should be fairly moist.

4 Lightly butter a microwave-proof plastic basin 1.2–1.5 litres (2–2$\frac{1}{2}$ pints) and put a circle of greaseproof paper in the base. Tip the mixture into the basin and smooth the top. Cover with microwave film or ordinary cling film, which has been pierced with a skewer.

5 Cook for 20 minutes on low in a 650 watt microwave oven. (Do check the power rating of the microwave oven and adjust the times accordingly.) Leave to stand for 5 minutes.

6 To serve, run a knife around the edges of the basin and turn out onto a warmed serving plate. To flame the pudding, put 2 tablespoons of brandy into a glass and microwave on full power for 30 seconds. Pour over the pudding and light immediately. Serve with Brandy Butter.

Freezing recommended

MEW

GRAN'S CHRISTMAS PUDDING

Christmas Puddings have endless permutations of ingredients and most families will have a traditional recipe. The origin of this one is unknown. It is very rich and moist, particularly if made one to two months ahead to allow time for the flavours to develop. **Serves 8–10**
Preparation time: 1 hour + 6–8 hours initial cooking

125 g (4½ oz) ready to eat prunes, chopped
225 g (8 oz) raisins
225 g (8 oz) currants
225 g (8 oz) sultanas
50 g (2 oz) mixed candied peel (preferably in large pieces), chopped rind and juice of 1 lemon
50 g (2 oz) chopped almonds
1 cooking apple approximately 125 g (4½ oz), peeled, cored and grated
1 medium carrot 75 g (2¾ oz) peeled and grated
225 g (8 oz) molasses sugar
225 g (8 oz) suet (I use vegetable rather than beef)
125 g (4½ oz) fresh white breadcrumbs
125 g (4½ oz) plain flour

½ teaspoon ground cinnamon
½ teaspoon ground coriander
½ teaspoon freshly ground nutmeg
3 eggs
150 ml (¼ pint) strong ale
1 tablespoon black treacle

1 In bowl one put the first nine ingredients in the list and mix together.

2 In bowl two put the next seven ingredients and mix together.

3 Mix together the contents of bowls one and two. The easiest way to do this is with very clean hands.

4 In a basin put the eggs and ale and whisk together and stir into the mixture. Stir in the black treacle.

5 Cover and leave to stand overnight in a cool place.

6 Butter the pudding basin and put a circle of greaseproof paper in the base.

7 Pack the mixture into the basin and smooth the top. Leave a 2.5 cm (1 inch) head space.

8 Cut a double layer of greaseproof paper or baking parchment into a 33 cm (13 inch) circle. Make a pleat and cover the pudding. Tie with string around the edge, then tie with more string and make a handle so that it can be easily lifted in and out of the pan.

9 Put the basin in the top of a steamer of simmering water and steam for the required time.

Remember to top up with boiling water every hour.

10 Put the basin on a trivet (or an upturned saucer) in a large heavy-based saucepan. Pour boiling water around the edge until it comes ²/₃ of the way up the side of the bowl. Cover with the lid of the pan and simmer for the required time. Remember to top up with boiling water every hour.

11 Cool. Put on a new greaseproof or parchment cover, and then cover tightly with foil.

12 Store in a cool dark place until Christmas. It will keep for up to 6 months.

13 Steam for 2 hours before serving.

14 Turn out on to a warm serving plate. Warm 2 tablespoons of rum in a small saucepan. Set alight and carefully pour over the pudding. Place a sprig of holly on the top and serve.

 Freezing not recommended

Tip: This mixture can be divided to make one 1.2 litre (2 pints) and one 600 ml (1 pint) puddng. Steaming times will be 4–6 hours and 2–3 hours respectively.

MEW

BRANDY BUTTER

Brandy Butter served with Christmas pudding and mince pies is part and parcel of Christmas. It is incredibly quick and easy to make so there's no need to pay inflated supermarket prices! **Serves 6** Preparation time: 5 minutes

115 g (4 oz) unsalted butter, softened
115 g (4 oz) light muscovado sugar
3–4 tablespoons brandy

1 Place the butter and sugar in a bowl and cream together until smooth and the mixture is light and fluffy.
2 Stir in the brandy and spoon into a serving bowl. Refrigerate the butter until ready to use.

❄ *Freezing recommended*

SCC

RUM SAUCE

This sweet white sauce, made in the same way as a roux, is an alternative to the more traditional brandy butter. It can be frozen but I prefer to make it between courses on Christmas day. It gives everyone a breather; the adults finish off the wine and the children pull more crackers, and then we all enjoy the Christmas Pud and Rum Sauce. **Serves 6–8** Preparation time: 25 minutes

50 g (2 oz) butter
50 g (2 oz) flour
600 ml (1 pint) milk
50 g (2 oz) unrefined caster sugar
3 tablespoons dark rum (more if desired)

1 Make a roux with the butter and flour: melt the butter in a saucepan, blend in the flour and cook over a low heat for 2–3 minutes, stirring constantly with a wooden spoon. It will look 'sandy' in texture.
2 Remove the pan from the heat and gradually add the milk to the roux, which will at first thicken to a solid mass.
3 Beat until the mixture leaves the sides of the pan clean, and then add a little more milk. Allow the mixture to thicken and boil between each addition of milk. Continuous beating is essential to produce a smooth sauce.
4 When all the milk has been added, bring the sauce to the boil and simmer for about 5 minutes.
5 Stir in the sugar and rum to taste and heat through gently.
6 Pour the sauce into a warm jug to serve.

❄ *Freezing: Pour into a container, seal and freeze. Thaw overnight.*

Tip: To prevent a skin forming on top of the sauce, cover it with a piece of damp greaseproof paper or cling film.

All-in-one method: A basic white sauce can also be made by the 'all-in-one' method. Put fat, flour and milk into a saucepan. Cook over a low heat, whisking all the time until the sauce thickens. Boil for 3 minutes then add flavouring.

MEW

CHRISTMAS CARDS

Most people will appreciate the thought and effort that goes into making your own cards and here are just a few simple ideas to make them a success.

Collage cards

You will need:
- paper for card
- a variety of fabrics and papers
- glue

You could layer a variety of different fabrics and papers to make a small collage. These could include some of the following: Christmas patchwork fabrics with tiny motifs, tissue paper, handmade papers, brown paper, coloured cellophane, corrugated card or felt. Now add a decoration on top of your layers of paper – this could be a leaf, a stamped motif, a pretty button or beads or anything else appropriate for the recipient of the gift. Try to think of a colour scheme and use materials in shades of the same colour.

Motif cards

You will need:
- paper for card
- glitter and paint or glue

or
- needle and thread
- sequins

or
- coloured pens or beads
- fabric scarf
- buttons

You could decorate your cards in the same way as your wrapping paper (page 37). If you made a star motif, add some glitter to the paint or glue or stitch some sequins or beads to the centre and the points. You could use the same idea to add jewels to a crown motif or decorations to a Christmas tree.

Alternatively you could design a different printing block and mark it over the top. For example you could try a snowman and then fill in the eyes, nose and mouth with coloured pens or stick small beads on. You could add a fabric scarf and use real buttons at the front.

Cards with inserts

You will need:
- paper for card
- insert of your choice
- glue or needle and ribbon or card

Inserts look rather special, and they can either be glued down the fold in the card or you could make tiny holes with a fine needle and tie them in place with a ribbon or fine cord.

Shapes

You will need:
- paper for card
- children's scissors (optional)

You could make cards in different shapes as an alternative to square or rectangular cards. First work out whether they will stand up by making a template from a piece of paper and then cut it out in card. Another idea is to cut out the card with children's scissors. These are available with a variety of interesting edges from most toy shops.

AG

STAR MINCE PIES

Christmas wouldn't be the same without mince pies. While they are readily available in the shops, they're rarely a patch on home-made ones. I gave some of these to Ruth, a friend, who commented on how good they were – she'd forgotten how much better home-made mince pies are because she was used to shop-bought ones. If you make mince pies well in advance and freeze them, it's best to put them in the freezer uncooked – this way you can just pop them in the oven from frozen (you will need to add a few minutes to the cooking time) when your guests arrive. They won't be able to resist a mince pie or two straight from the oven! **Makes 18–20**
Preparation time: 30 minutes + 30 minutes chilling + cooling
Cooking time: 20 minutes

225 g (8 oz) plain flour
115 g (4 oz) butter, diced
50 g (2 oz) lard, cut into small pieces
25 g (1 oz) icing sugar
1 egg, lightly beaten
2 teaspoons iced water
450 g (1 lb) Luxury Mincemeat (see page 26)

1 To make the pastry sift the flour into a bowl and add the butter and lard. Rub the fats into the flour until the mixture resembles breadcrumbs. Stir in the icing sugar and then add the egg and water. Bring together to form a smooth dough. This can be done with ease in the food processor – however, do be careful when you add the water as you are unlikely to need so much.

2 Place in a plastic bag and refrigerate for half an hour.

3 Preheat the oven to Gas Mark 4/electric oven 180°C/fan oven 160°C.

4 Roll out just over half the pastry to about 3 mm ($\frac{1}{8}$ inch) thickness and cut out circles large enough to fit the base of the tart tins. You will need to re-roll the off cuts. Fill with mincemeat, making sure you don't add too much or it will spill out of the pastry during cooking.

5 Roll out the remaining pastry and cut out tops for the mince pies – I like to use a star-shaped cutter because it makes the pies look so attractive. Place the stars on top and lightly press down the points onto the pastry bases.

6 Bake in the oven for 15–20 minutes until the mince pies are golden brown. Allow them to cool in the tins for a few minutes and then transfer them to a cooling rack to finish cooling.

7 Dust with icing sugar and serve with Brandy Butter (page 22).

Freezing: Place the uncooked mince pies, still in the tins, into the freezer. When frozen, place the trays into large freezer bags – supermarket carrier bags are fine if they're not going to be in the freezer for long. Cook from frozen but remember to add a few minutes to the cooking time.

SCC

DECORATED CANDLES

This works best with non-drip, unpainted candles because you can remove any mistakes without damaging the paint. Decorating candles is easy, but as you will be using a hot glue gun take care, especially if children are around. The glue dries very quickly, and you can obtain a variety of different effects, depending on the type of glue and candle you use.

You will need:

- candles
- a hot glue gun
- hot glue glitter sticks (available from a craft shop, especially at Christmas time)

1 Heat the glue stick.
2 When it has heated up, you can either make a pattern or simply scribble over the candle.
3 Avoid decorating the base and the wick, and leave enough room at the bottom of the candle so that it fits into its holder.

LUXURY MINCEMEAT

There are so many recipes for mincemeat, but this is my version and has become a firm favourite with the family over the years. It is easy to make, can be used straight from the freezer (it scoops like soft ice cream) and keeps for up to 6 months.

Makes approximately 1.5 kg (3$\frac{1}{2}$ lb 5 oz) Preparation time: 25 minutes + cooling Cooking time: 30 minutes

125 g (4$\frac{1}{2}$ oz) raisins
125 g (4$\frac{1}{2}$ oz) sultanas
125 g (4$\frac{1}{2}$ oz) currants
125 g (4$\frac{1}{2}$ oz) ready to eat figs, chopped
125 g (4$\frac{1}{2}$ oz) ready to eat dates, chopped
175 g (6 oz) unrefined dark Muscovado sugar
75 g (2$\frac{3}{4}$ oz) butter
1 teaspoon ground cinnamon
1 teaspoon freshly ground nutmeg
1 teaspoon ground cloves
450 g (1 lb) peeled, cored and diced cooking apples (see tip)
150 ml (¼ pint) cider
grated rind and juice of 1 lemon
2 tablespoons syrup
2 tablespoons brandy
2 tablespoons Madeira
50 g (2 oz) chopped nuts (hazelnuts or walnut)

1 Mix all the dried fruit, sugar, butter, spices and apples in a bowl.
2 Heat the cider in a large pan until it bubbles around the edge.
3 Stir in the fruit mixture, lemon rind and juice, and syrup.
4 Cover and simmer for 20 minutes, stirring occasionally. Remove the lid and continue to simmer until the juice is almost absorbed.
5 Cool; stir in the brandy, Madeira and nuts.

Freezing: Put in a rigid container, seal and label.

Tip: When making shortcrust pastry for mince pies, add to the basic ingredients the grated rind of one orange and 100 g (3$\frac{1}{2}$ oz) of golden icing sugar and substitute the orange juice for some of the water.

It is essential to have 450 g (1 lb) apples after the peel and cores have been removed.

MEW

TASSELS

These make good tree decorations or they can be used to decorate wrapped Christmas presents.

1 To make a tassel, take a piece of card (an old cereal packet is ideal) about 1 cm (½ inch) longer than you want the finished tassel to be and cut a slot in one end. Put the end of the thread in the slot. Now wrap the card with the thread until you have the fullness you want.

2 Take a piece of thread, about 30 cm (12 inches) long and fold it in half. Pass this thread under the threads at one end of the card, take the two ends through the loop and pull tight.

3 Now remove the tassel from the card and wrap some more threads about a third of the way down to make the head of the tassel. Make sure these threads are tied off well and the ends are buried in the head.

4 Cut through the loops at the bottom of the tassel (the skirt) and trim them evenly. Give the tassel a good shake to fluff it out.

To make a beaded tassel:
The simplest way of incorporating beads into a tassel is to pick them up on the thread that you use for tying under the loop in step 3. You may need to secure the top without beads to start off with and then add them on another thread afterwards.

or:
Another way is to make a beaded skirt. To do this, before you start wrapping the thread, pick up the same number of beads as you are going to do wraps around the card. Each time you wrap the thread around the card, 'drop' a bead off at one end, then continue until you have no more beads. Finish the tassel as before but don't trim the skirt.

CHRISTMAS STOLLEN

Stollen is a sweet festive bread from Germany. This recipe makes two loaves so you can follow the German tradition of making one to keep and one to give. Use a food processor to remove the hard work of kneading, as well as a bread mix, available from most supermarkets. **Makes 2 loaves**, 16 slices each Preparation time: 20 minutes + 40–45 minutes proving + overnight soaking and cooling Cooking time: 25–30 minutes

500 g (1 lb 2 oz) pack of white bread mix

100 g (3½ oz) butter, diced

50 g (2 oz) unrefined castor sugar

1 egg, lightly beaten

250 ml (9 fl oz) warm water

2 teaspoons almond essence

2 teaspoons vanilla essence

grated rind of 1 lemon

100 g (3½ oz) dried apricots, chopped finely

100 g (3½ oz) sultanas

100 g (3½ oz) raisins

100 g (3½ oz) mixed peel (preferably chopped yourself) to contain orange, lemon and citron

3 tablespoons dark rum

25 g (1 oz) whole almonds, blanched and chopped

50 g (2 oz) glacé cherries, cut into quarters

225 g (8 oz) white marzipan

To finish:

50 g (2 oz) melted butter

icing sugar, for dusting

1 Soak the apricots, sultanas, raisins and mixed peel in rum overnight.

2 Mix in the nuts and lemon rind.

3 Put the butter, sugar and bread mix into a food processor bowl fitted with a dough attachment. Mix for 1 or 2 minutes until the butter is incorporated.

4 Blend the almond and vanilla essence with 250 ml (9 fl oz) warm water and add, together with the beaten egg, to the bowl. Mix for 5 minutes to form a dough and then rest the dough for 5 minutes.

5 Add the dried fruit soaked in rum, nuts and lemon rind and mix into the dough.

6 Remove the dough from the bowl on to a floured surface. Knead until smooth then divide it and reshape it into two rounds. Rest the dough for 5 minutes.

7 Divide the marzipan into two pieces and roll each into a sausage shape.

8 Pat out each piece of dough with the heel of the hand to form a 20 cm (8 inch) round. Place the marzipan slightly off-centre on the dough. Sprinkle each half with the cherries.

9 Brush over the surface of the dough with water to moisten, then fold the smaller side over the marzipan to cover it and leave a ledge of dough.

10 Cover the dough with a clean tea towel or lightly oiled plastic film and leave in a warm place for 40–45 minutes or until doubled in size.

11 Bake in preheated oven at Gas mark 6/electric oven 200°C/fan oven 180°C for 25–30 minutes or until golden brown. To test if it is cooked, give the base a sharp tap – it should sound hollow when it is done.

12 Remove the bread from the oven and drench it with melted butter, making sure it soaks in between each application – this helps to keep the dough fresh for longer. Cool the stollen on a wire rack. Dust heavily with icing sugar.

13 The stollen can be frozen for up to 1 month.

Freezing : do not dust with icing sugar before you do; instead, wrap it in greaseproof paper and foil and then freeze. To thaw, keep at room temperature overnight and then dust with icing sugar.

Tip: To prepare as a gift, tie a ribbon around the stollen like a parcel and wrap it in cellophane.

MEW

SCOTTISH SHORTBREAD

This is an old Scottish recipe given to me by a neighbour and it has been handed down through her family for generations. Butter is the essential ingredient that gives the shortbread its smooth creamy flavour. The mixture was originally made by hand but nowadays a food processor will speed up the preparation. **Makes 16 pieces** Preparation time: 15 minutes + cooling Cooking time: 1 hour

You will need two 18 cm
(7 inch) fluted round tins with
loose bases
225 g (8 oz) slightly salted butter
cut into pieces
150 g (5 oz) sieved icing sugar
300 g (10 oz) plain flour
75 g (2¾ oz) cornflour
caster sugar, for sprinkling

1 Put the butter and icing sugar into the food processor bowl, fitted with the multi-purpose blade and pulse, until they are combined together.

2 Add the flour and cornflour and continue to process until the mixture forms a ball.

3 Turn out onto a lightly floured surface and knead gently until smooth.

4 Divide the dough in half, pat into two rounds and roll each out to an 18 cm (7 inch) circle.

5 Transfer the shortbread rounds to the tins and press the mixture evenly into the fluted edges.

6 Prick the surface of the dough all over with a fork and mark out into eight equal pieces with a knife, not cutting all the way through. Preheat the oven to Gas Mark 3/160°C/fan oven 140°C.

7 Bake for 1 hour. The shortbread should be very pale and feel firm in the centre.

8 While the shortbread is still warm, cut through the markings and sprinkle with caster sugar. Leave to cool in the tins.

7 Remove the shortbread when it is cold and store in an airtight tin.

To present the shortbread as a gift, cut a circle of stiff card to fit the size of the shortbread base. Lay two pieces of tartan ribbon in a cross on the underside of the card and stick in place. Turn the card over, arrange the shortbread on it and then tie the ribbon in a bow. Wrap in clear cellophane.

 Freezing not recommended

MEW

SPECIAL MILLIONAIRE CHOCOLATE SQUARES

I have loved millionaire shortbread for such a long time but rarely make it as it's quite time-consuming. I decided to try and cheat a little by using banoffee sauce instead of boiling condensed milk and combining it with plain chocolate to get the right texture (chocolate firms as it sets). I was thrilled with the result! **Makes 15**
Preparation time: 30 minutes
Cooking time: 20 minutes

175 g (6 oz) plain flour
115 g (4 oz) butter, diced
50 g (2 oz) soft brown sugar
345 g bottle of banoffee sauce
115 g (4 oz) plain chocolate, broken into squares
150 g (5 oz) white chocolate, broken into squares

1 Preheat the oven to Gas Mark 5/ electric 190°C/fan oven 170°C. Grease a 23 cm (9 inch) square cake tin.
2 Place the flour and butter in a bowl and rub in the butter until the mixture resembles breadcrumbs. Add the sugar, stir in and bring the mixture together to form a dough. Press the dough into the prepared tin and prick it (all over) with a fork.
3 Bake in the oven for 20 minutes until lightly golden. Allow to cool in the tin.
4 Place the banoffee sauce and plain chocolate in a saucepan and melt over a very gentle heat. Remove from the heat and spread over the shortbread. Allow to set in a cool place for at least two hours.
5 Melt the white chocolate over a bowl of hot water and then spread it over the banoffee filling. Leave it to virtually set and then mark out 15 squares. When it has set completely, cut into the squares.

Freezing recommended
Open freeze and then place in a freezer bag. To thaw, simply take the required number of squares and thaw them at room temperature on the serving plate.

SCC

GINGERBREAD MEN

I suppose in these politically correct times, these delicious biscuits should be renamed Gingerbread people! Gingerbread people are traditional tree decorations. Before baking, make a small hole in the top of their heads and when they are cooked you can tie a ribbon through the hole and hang them on the tree. It is some consolation for the children when the tree comes down to have a treat of gingerbread to eat.

Gingerbread people can also be used as an advent calendar treat throughout December. The idea is that you ice 24 gingerbread boys and girls and then add a number, from 1–24, on their tummies. Wrap them up and put one in the child's lunchbox each day as a countdown to Christmas. To ensure that they are always fresh. you need to make several batches (perhaps 5 or 6 at a time) throughout December

They are traditionally made with syrup but I make them using half syrup and half treacle which, in addition to giving them a deeper colour, gives them a wonderful flavour. *Makes about 20 Preparation and cooking times: 40 minutes*

butter, for greasing
350 g (12 oz) plain flour
1 teaspoon bicarbonate of soda
2 teaspoons ground ginger
½ teaspoon ground cinnamon
115 g (4 oz) butter, cubed
175 g (6 oz) light muscovado sugar
2 tablespoons golden syrup
2 tablespoons treacle
1 egg, beaten
To decorate
currants
**stiff glacé icing or a tube of
   supercook writing icing (optional)**

1 Preheat the oven to Gas Mark 5/electric 190°C/fan oven 170°C.
2 Lightly grease two large baking sheets or line with baking parchment paper.
3 Sift the flour, bicarbonate of soda and spices into a large bowl. Add the butter and rub in until the mixture resembles breadcrumbs. Add the sugar and stir in. Add the syrup, treacle and egg to the mixture and bring together to form a smooth dough.

4 Divide the dough in half and roll out one piece on a lightly floured board to about 5 mm (¼ inch) thickness. Cut into gingerbread people using a cutter and place them onto the baking sheet. Repeat with the remaining dough and then use the currants for eyes and buttons.
5 Bake in the oven for 10–12 minutes until they are a bit darker in colour. Cool for a couple of minutes and then transfer them to a cooling rack to cool completely.
6 Decorate with icing, if using.

❄ *Freezing not recommended*

Tip: Don't be tempted to leave the biscuits in the oven for any longer than stated as they will become too hard as they cool.

SCC

CHRISTMAS CINNAMON STARS

These can be hung on the Christmas tree as an attractive decoration. Use a skewer to make a hole of about 1 cm (½ inch) from the edge of each biscuit. When baked, thread a ribbon or cord through the holes, tie in a loop and hang them from the tree. **Makes 20 to 24** Preparation time: 20 minutes + Chilling 10 minutes + Cooking time: 15–20 minutes

175 g (6 oz) unsalted butter, softened

125 g (4½ oz) unrefined light soft brown sugar

225 g (8 oz) self-raising flour

½ teaspoon mixed spice

1 teaspoon ground cinnamon

grated rind of 1 lemon

50 g (2 oz) almonds, blanched and chopped

25 g (1 oz) digestive biscuits, crushed

For the glacé icing

225 g (8 oz) icing sugar, sieved

silver balls, to decorate

1 Cream the butter and sugar together until light and fluffy. Sift the flour, mixed spice and cinnamon, then add the lemon rind, nuts and biscuit crumbs. Bind the ingredients together to make a firm dough.

2 On a lightly floured work surface, roll out the dough to a depth of 8 mm (⅜ inch) then cut out the biscuits using a star biscuit cutter.

3 Line the baking trays with sheets of parchment paper or black Teflon squares. Place the biscuits on baking trays and chill for 10 minutes. Bake at Gas Mark 4/electric oven 180°C/fan oven 160°C for 15–20 minutes until they are golden brown.

4 Leave for a few minutes to harden then transfer the biscuits to a wire rack to cool.

5 Store in an airtight tin.

6 To decorate, make up the glacé icing by beating the icing sugar and 2 tablespoons warm water together until it is a smooth consistency and coats the back of a wooden spoon. Spread the icing onto the biscuits with a palette knife and place a silver ball at the point of each star. Leave to harden.

Freezing recommended Freezing: Freeze undecorated; pack into a rigid container, seal and label.

MEW

WRAPPING EDIBLE GIFTS

People really love to receive edible gifts – they appreciate that they are a labour of love as time and effort has gone into preparing something just for them rather than a present chosen in a shop. Homemade food is considered a real treat these days as so much convenience food is eaten. Not only are these gifts popular, they are memorable too.

Labelling food presents is important – you need to give plenty of information about how it should be stored and for how long, together with the date it was made.

Once your gifts are made, it is worth spending time to wrap them attractively. The wrapping doesn't have to be complicated or time-consuming, just carefully chosen to suit the person receiving the gift. The particular type of wrapping will of course be determined by the contents of the present and whether or not it will be hand delivered or posted. Attractive boxes, jars and bottles are great, and look especially nice when encased in festive wrapping. Wrapping gifts imaginatively and individually makes them special.

This is a good opportunity to involve younger members of your family, even if it takes longer and gets a little messy! It gives them the chance to be creative – and perhaps they will be inspired to make presents for teachers and friends, such as decorative candles, biscuits or tree decorations. They might even like to make a centrepiece for the table.

WRAPPING PAPER

The first of these two ideas is nice to do with young children, who can decorate papers to wrap presents for friends or family.

You will need:
- brown paper (it will take any colour of paint and still look good)
- half a potato or star fruit
- metallic paint (for method 1) or gold or silver paint (for method 2)
- gift tags or Christmas cards (optional)

1 Pick a simple motif, such as stars or Christmas trees, that will be easy to cut out and will work well with just one colour.
2 Trace it onto a piece of paper, to make a template, and lay it on half a potato.
3 Draw around the outline and cut into the potato with a sharp knife to make a block for printing. Alternatively, you could cut a star fruit in thick slices and use these. Use metallic paint to stamp randomly all over the brown paper, If you wish, you could add one motif on a gift tag or on the front of a homemade Christmas card.
or
1 Another way of decorating paper is to spray over the template. You could use the paper Christmas snowflakes on page 17.
2 Lay the snowflakes on the paper and spray with gold or silver paint. Don't worry too much about gaps or getting a solid colour background; it is the mottled effect that makes the paper individual.

RIBBONS

Ribbons can be used to tie decorations onto trees, wrap presents or enhance floral arrangements.

A variety of traditional ribbons can be bought from craft shops and haberdashery departments, together with beautifully coloured organza ribbons, paper ribbons and some with wired edges so that they will hold the shape of a bow more easily.

Consider using other things for tying. If you have decorated brown paper for your presents, why not use raffia? This can be bought in neutral or various colours to tie in with your colour scheme. Another option is to make a plait from different colours of string.

Lengths of lace can also be used as ties and these are available in a range of widths and colours. If you can't find the colour you are looking for, cotton lace can be dyed very easily. To add a sparkle to the wrapping, use sequins, which can be bought on a string.

To make a cord
You will need:
- narrow ribbons, threads or wools
or
1 Make a cord by tying a bunch of threads together in a loop about three times the length of the finished cord.
2 Place one end over a hook (or get a friend to hold it for you) and put a pencil through the end with the knot.
3 Use the pencil to twist the cord as tightly as you can and without letting go bring the ends together and watch the threads twist into a cord.
4 You will need to straighten out the cord before knotting the ends and cutting off any loose threads.

23rd and 24th December

We think the couple of days before Christmas are so exciting. The anticipation of the big day is wonderful. The final preparations – cooking some of the festive dishes, wrapping presents and making the decorations for the table – can begin. As a child, the excitement was almost unbearable!

Christmas for us really begins on Christmas Eve. When we were at home with our families, we used to listen to the Nine Lessons and Carols on the radio and then we went to Midnight Mass.

The more you can do in the run up to Christmas, when you are under less pressure, the better. Then you can enjoy a more relaxing Christmas Day. With this in mind, we have created the recipes on the following pages. Margaret has created some deliciously different recipes using familiar and traditional, as well as unusual, ingredients, such as the Cranberry and Kumquat Sauce and Honey and Fig Baked Ham. She has created two stuffing recipes for you to choose from. The sweet recipes I have produced include a trifle using seasonal and convenience ingredients and other alternatives to Christmas Pudding – a chocolate log, ice cream and a compote. On Christmas or Boxing Day, these just need to be reheated, presented on plates or simply served – what could be easier?

Christmas trifle (page 56)

HONEY AND FIG BAKED HAM

A traditional glazed ham is perfect for the festive season and useful for serving large numbers of people. Serve it hot for a meal on Christmas Eve and then use the leftovers as cold cuts for the buffet table and sandwiches. Don't forget the ham bone, which will make a wonderful stock for soup.

I have included several ways to cook the gammon and ideas for different glazes to finish the ham but my favourite has its origin in Roman times when a gammon would have been baked, with honey and figs, in an olive oil and flour pastry crust. However, I use a foil parcel instead.

Choosing a gammon joint: gammon is the cured hind leg of the (bacon) pig. When it is cooked, it is called ham. It is available smoked or unsmoked.

To soak or not? Soaking removes excess salt. If the joint has been mild-cured then it will not need soaking. To soak, place the joint in a large bowl covered with water and leave for 24 hours or overnight, then discard water. Alternatively, place the joint in a pan of cold water and bring to the boil. Remove the scum and discard the water immediately. Continue with one of the cooking methods below.

Serves 8 with enough for leftovers Preparation time: 30 minutes + 24 hours or overnight soaking if required Cooking time: 2–3 hours depending on size and method

Cooking method

Boiling: 20 minutes per 450 g (1 lb)

Boiling and baking: boil the joint for half the calculated cooking time. Remove from the hot liquid and place in a roasting tin. Cover with foil and cook at Gas Mark 4/ electric oven 180°C/fan oven 160°C for the remainder of the cooking time, less 20 minutes. Remove the foil and glaze to finish.

Baking: with the added flavourings and liquid, wrap the joint in a loose parcel using extra-wide and strong foil. Bake at Gas Mark 4/electric oven 180°C/fan oven 160°C for 2–3 hours.

225 g (8 oz) dried figs

4–6 bay leaves

3–4 shallots, peeled and halved

2.7–3.6 kg (6–8 lb) joint of gammon

2 tablespoons honey

300 ml (½ pint) wine or cider

To glaze ham

50 g (2 oz) honey

75 g (2¾ oz) unrefined soft brown sugar

150 ml (2¾ pint) cooking liquid

Garnish

6–8 fresh figs, halved

1 tablespoon honey

1–2 oranges, sliced finely

bay leaves

1 Soak the gammon if necessary *(see recipe introduction)*. Place a large sheet of foil in a roasting tin and on it make a bed of dried figs, bay leaves and shallots. Place the joint on top and then spread the skin with honey. Pour over the wine or cider. Cover the joint with another layer of foil and seal the edges together, leaving enough room inside for the steam to surround the ham. Cook as for baking.

2 To glaze, open the parcel, remove the skin and score across the fat in a diamond pattern. Mix the glaze ingredients together and brush over the ham.

3 Return to the oven and bake for 15–20 minutes, basting once. Leave the ham to cool. If freezing, do so at this point.

4 To make the garnish, brush the figs and orange skins with honey. Heat a little olive oil in a frying pan, add the figs (cut-side down) and oranges, and cook for 2–3 minutes until caramelised.

5 To serve, transfer the ham to a warm serving plate and place the garnish, with bay leaves, around the edge.

Alternative ideas for glazing:

• Stud the ham with cloves

• 3 tablespoons of honey, 1 tablespoon of mustard and the juice of 1 orange

• 2 tablespoons of honey, 2 tablespoons of wine vinegar, 50 g (2 oz) demerara sugar and 50 g (2 oz) breadcrumbs

• 100g (3½ oz) dark Oxford or thick ginger marmalade

• 50 g (2 oz) mixed oatmeal and 50 g (2 oz) brown sugar

• 50 g (2 oz) ground coffee, a pinch of mustard, 100 g (3½ oz) brown sugar, mixed to a paste with a little water

• 2 tablespoons of quince or redcurrant jelly, 1 tablespoon of whole grain mustard, ½ teaspoon allspice and ½ teaspoon coriander.

 *Freezing: when cold, either wrap the ham in foil or place in a large freezer bag. To thaw, leave in the refrigerator overnight.*

MEW

HAMPERS

Gift baskets and food hampers are usually expensive and they often contain a certain number of things we don't really want.

It is easy to make your own hamper, and it's a good idea to buy small presents throughout the year to spread the cost. Take time to shop around too. The more personal you can make your hamper, the better. It is also a good idea to stick to a colour scheme as this makes the whole effect more professional.

Think of using terracotta pots, crammed full of bulbs or packets of seeds for the gardener, a selection of unusual food items for the gourmet (remember to check the expiry dates), a selection of beauty products for the teenage girl, or make up some of the recipes in this book and pack them as a gift for an elderly friend or relative.

Consider whether you are going to wrap individual gifts because this can be time consuming. It is often just as effective to arrange them in something appropriate which can also be used as a gift: try straw (easily obtainable from pet shops) for the gardener, a tea towel for the cook, and a pretty hand towel for the teenager. If the basket does not have a lid, wrap the whole basket in cellophane and tie it with a gift bow.

AG

SMOKED SALMON & GARLIC MOUSSE WITH SLICED CUCUMBER & DILL DRESSING

Smoked salmon is still something of a luxury and this perfect starter never fails to impress. Although it takes a little time to prepare, it is well worth the effort. It freezes well and so can be made in advance. If you don't have a ring mould, use a loaf tin instead. **Serves 8–10** Preparation time: 45 minutes + chilling + 1½ hours freezing.

Smoked Salmon and Garlic Mousse

200 g (7 oz) pack sliced smoked salmon
2 x 200 g (7 oz) cartons of soft cheese with garlic and herbs
1 garlic clove, crushed
150 ml (5 fl oz) carton of soured cream
2 eggs, separated
1 tablespoon powdered gelatine
5 cm (2 inches) cucumber, diced finely
175 g (6 oz) smoked salmon trimmings

1 teaspoon sun-dried tomato paste
oil, for greasing
salt and freshly ground black pepper

Cucumber and dill dressing
1 small cucumber, skin removed, sliced into thin strips
3 tablespoons olive oil
1 tablespoon white wine vinegar
1 teaspoon caster sugar
2 tablespoons chopped fresh dill
salt and freshly ground black pepper

1 Lightly oil an 850 ml (1½ pint) ring mould and line with cling film. Use 100 g (3½ oz) thinly sliced smoked salmon and line the base. Chill.

2 Meanwhile, put the soft cheese, garlic, soured cream, 2 egg yolks, salt and pepper into a processor and blend until smooth.

3 Sprinkle gelatine over 4 tablespoons of cold water in a small basin and leave for 2–3 minutes until sponge-like. Dissolve over a pan of simmering water or heat for 30 seconds in a microwave oven. The end result must be a pale straw-coloured liquid. Pour into the cheese mixture and blend in. Don't worry that the mixture seems very runny at this stage. Pour 175 ml (6 fl oz) into a small bowl and stir in the diced cucumber. Cover and leave at room temperature. Add the smoked salmon trimmings to the remaining mixture in the processor

with the tomato purée and blend again until smooth. Put into a mixing bowl.

4 Lightly whisk the egg whites until stiff. Fold 2 tablespoons into the cucumber cheese mixture and the remainder into the smoked salmon mixture.

5 Spoon half the smoked salmon mixture into the base of the ring mould and place in a freezer to set (approximately 10–15 minutes). Remove from the freezer, add the remaining 100 g (3½ oz) slices of salmon in a layer, then the cucumber cheese mixture, and freeze again for approximately 10 minutes. Spoon over the remaining salmon mixture, cover and freeze for 1 hour.

6 To make the dressing, peel and slice the cucumber into long strips, sprinkle with salt and leave for 30 minutes. Squeeze out the moisture and pat dry. Make up the vinaigrette dressing by putting all the ingredients into a jam jar and shaking well to combine. Pour over the cucumber and chill until required.

7 To serve, turn the mousse out onto a flat plate and leave to soften for about 45 minutes. Slice into portions and serve with the cucumber and dill dressing and salad leaves.

Freezing recommended

MEW

SPICED CREAM OF WATERCRESS SOUP WITH CHEESY CROUTONS

With its peppery taste, watercress is always a popular soup choice and can be enjoyed either hot or cold. In 1616 the herbalist Culpeper stated that watercress was very effective at cleansing the blood so perhaps this is the ideal soup to counteract all the rich food of Christmas. **Serves 4–6**
Preparation time: 20 minutes
Cooking time 25 minutes

2 bundles or 2 x 85 g (3 oz)
    prepared packs of watercress
50 g (2 oz) butter
1 medium onion, peeled and diced
2 medium potatoes 225 g (8 oz),
    peeled and diced
3 teaspoons ground coriander
1 litre (1¾ pints) chicken or
    vegetable stock
300 ml (½ pint) single cream
salt and pepper
Croutons
1 slice of medium-thick white
    bread, crusts removed
1 tablespoon olive oil
1 tablespoon finely grated cheese,
    such as Parmesan
½ teaspoon ground coriander

1 Chop the watercress after reserving a few leaves for garnish.
2 Melt the butter in a large saucepan. Add the onion, potatoes and coriander and cook gently with the lid on, for about 3–4 minutes, stirring occasionally. Do not brown. Add the watercress and cook until wilted. Season with salt and pepper.
3 Add the stock, stir and bring to the boil, then simmer for about 20 minutes or until the vegetables are soft. Cool slightly.
4 Liquidise. Return the soup to the pan, taste and adjust the seasoning.
5 Add the cream and reheat gently.
6 To make croutons, preheat the oven to Gas Mark 4/electric oven 180°C/fan oven 160°C. Cut the bread into 1 cm (½ inch) cubes and mix with the rest of the ingredients.
7 Spread the bread cubes on a baking sheet and bake for 7–8 minutes until crisp and golden. The croutons can be made in advance and stored in an airtight tin.
8 To serve, garnish with the reserved watercress leaves, and a swirl of cream. Either serve the croutons separately or sprinkle on top of the soup.

Freezing: Complete to the end of stage 4 and then freeze in rigid containers.

MEW

CRANBERRY KUMQUAT SAUCE

Cranberries and orange complement each other and the use of kumquats is a new twist for this traditional sauce with turkey. This sauce is quick to make and is also excellent with cold meats, cheese and on canapés. **Serves 4** Preparation and cooking time: 35 minutes

225 g (8 oz) fresh cranberries
100 g (3½ oz) kumquats, halved
   and de-pipped
1 tablespoon fresh orange juice
cinnamon stick, approximately
   5 cm (2 inches) long
50 g (2 oz) muscovado sugar
2 tablespoons port

1 Put the cranberries, kumquats, orange juice and cinnamon stick into a saucepan with 150 ml (¼ pint) water. Bring to the boil and then simmer gently for about 10–15 minutes until the fruit is tender. Remove the cinnamon stick.
2 Add sugar and cook gently until it is dissolved.
3 Stir in the port and serve.

Freezing: Cool after stirring in the port, pack and freeze. To use, thaw overnight.

MEW

BREAD SAUCE

A roast turkey or chicken meal, particularly at Christmas, is incomplete without bread sauce. It is very straightforward to make, especially if you keep breadcrumbs in the freezer, as I do. **Makes 8 servings** Preparation and cooking time: 40 minutes + cooloing

1 medium onion, peeled
2–3 cloves
600 ml (1pint) milk
1 sprig of parsley
1 bay leaf
100 g (3½ oz) fresh white
   breadcrumbs
25 g (1 oz) butter
3 tablespoons single cream
salt and freshly ground black
   pepper

1 Pierce the onion with the cloves and place in a thick-bottomed saucepan with the milk, parsley and bay leaf.
2 Bring the milk to the boil slowly and then remove it from the heat, cover with a lid and leave to infuse for 10 minutes (longer, if time allows, for a really good flavour).
3 Remove the onion (with the cloves), parsley and bay leaf. Add the breadcrumbs and seasoning and bring to simmering point on a moderate heat. Simmer for 10–15 minutes, stirring from time to time.
4 Remove from the heat. Add the butter and stir to melt it, then stir in the cream.
5 Cool and then store, covered, in the fridge. Heat through before serving.

Freezing not recommended

Tip: To avoid getting a skin on the top of the sauce, put a couple of knobs of butter on the surface when heating through – the butter will melt and prevent a skin from forming.

SCC

CHESTNUT STUFFING

The Christmas turkey is traditionally stuffed with chestnuts. You can use fresh chestnuts but the recipe works just as well with pre-prepared chestnut pieces. **Serves 8** Preparation and cooking time: 25 minutes or 40 minutes if using fresh chestnuts

450 g (1 lb) whole chestnuts (optional, see step 1)
50 g (2 oz) onion, chopped finely
1 garlic clove, crushed
50 g (2 oz) streaky bacon, without rind, diced
50 g (2 oz) butter
175 g (6 oz) fresh white breadcrumbs
50 g (2 oz) suet
200 g (7 oz) pack of cooked and peeled chestnut pieces
2 tablespoons fresh parsley, chopped
½ teaspoon dried marjoram
½ teaspoon dried thyme
grated rind of 1 lemon
3 eggs, beaten
splash of milk or vegetable stock (optional)
salt and freshly ground black pepper

If using fresh chestnuts:

1 Split the skins and place the nuts under a hot grill until the skin can easily be peeled off. Put in a pan, cover with water and boil for 40 minutes until tender. Drain and roughly chop.

For the stuffing:

1 Fry the onions, garlic and bacon in butter and stir in the breadcrumbs and suet, then the chestnuts, herbs, and lemon rind. Continue to cook for a few minutes.

2 Remove from the heat, mix in the eggs and season with salt and pepper. If the stuffing is dry, add some milk or stock to make it 'sticky'.

3 Use the stuffing to stuff the neck end of the turkey. Any left over can be made into balls and baked separately.

Freezing: Pack into a container and freeze. To serve separately, form the stuffing into balls and open freeze, then pack.

MCC

SAGE, ONION AND PICKLED WALNUT STUFFING

This stuffing is excellent for complementing the fatty meat of goose. **Serves 8** Preparation and cooking time: 25 minutes

225 g (8 oz) onions, sliced thickly

goose liver

200 g (7 oz) fresh white
   breadcrumbs

50 g (2 oz) oatmeal (optional)

1 cooking apple, peeled cored and
   diced

100 g (3½ oz) ready-to-eat prunes,
   chopped

1 tablespoon dried sage

1 egg, beaten

juice and grated rind of 1 lemon

¼ teaspoon grated nutmeg

4–6 pickled walnuts, chopped
   roughly

salt and pepper

1 Cook the onions and the goose liver in a pan with sufficient water to cover. Bring to the boil and simmer for 4–5 minutes. Drain, remove the liver and chop finely.

2 Put the breadcrumbs, oatmeal, apple, prunes, onions and sage into a bowl and mix well, then season. Stir in the egg, lemon rind and juice, nutmeg, walnuts and liver. The mixture needs to be fairly dry as it will absorb some of the fat from the goose.

3 Use the stuffing to stuff the neck of the goose.

Freezing: Pack into a rigid container, seal and freeze. Thaw in the refrigerator.

MEW

ORGANZA BAG

These bags can go on a side plate, be strewn about the table or used for an edible gift, such as the Chocolate Fudge (opposite) or Chocolate Truffles (page 186).

You will need:
- a piece of organza the width of the finished bag and twice the length (you will need to add hems)
- needle
- thread
- gold ribbon or cord

1 To make the bag, turn down the top and bottom of the piece of organza, fold in half and sew up each side.

2 The top of the bag can then be tied around with a gold ribbon or cord.

AG

CHOCOLATE FUDGE

My husband gave this recipe the thumbs up – he normally finds fudge too sickly. He and Holly kept sneaking into the tin to have 'just one more piece'! The fudge makes a lovely gift, especially presented in an attractive box or bag. I used a hand-held electric whisk to make it as there is quite a lot of mixing involved. **Makes 80 pieces** Preparation and chilling time: 30 minutes + cooling minimum of 4 hours chilling

115 g (4 oz) butter, softened
1 teaspoon vanilla extract
405 g can condensed milk
115 g (4 oz) plain chocolate, broken into squares
800 g (1 lb 12 oz) icing sugar, sifted

1 Place the butter in a large bowl and beat in the vanilla extract and condensed milk.

2 Place the chocolate squares in a bowl and set it over a pan of barely simmering water. Leave it to melt, remove it from the heat and stir.

3 Allow the chocolate to cool and then beat it in, gradually, to the butter mixture. Beat in the icing sugar, a little at a time. When it has all been incorporated you should end up with a soft, dough-like mixture.

4 Line a 20 x 30 cm (8 x 12 inch) shallow baking tin with baking parchment paper. Press the fudge into the tin, ensuring that the surface is even. Using the tip of a sharp knife, mark the fudge into about 80 pieces and then place it in the fridge for at least 4 hours to set.

5 When the fudge has set, use the edges of the paper to lift it from the tin on to a large chopping board and cut it into the marked pieces. Place into the chosen gift boxes, but keep some for your family to enjoy!!

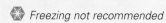 *Freezing not recommended*

SCC

CHOCOLATE LOG

This cake is quite rich and can be eaten at tea-time over Christmas or as a dessert. Since it contains fresh cream it should be stored in the fridge. It takes time to prepare but is well worth it as it is infinitely better than anything you can buy and will certainly impress your family and friends!. It freezes beautifully and so can be prepared well in advance.

Serves 10–12 Preparation time: 1 hour Cooking time: 15 minutes

4 eggs

150 g (5 oz) caster sugar plus extra for dusting

80 g (3 oz) plain flour

25 g (1 oz) cocoa powder

300 ml ($^1/_2$ pint) double cream

115 g (4 oz) plain chocolate, broken into pieces

225 g (8 oz) chestnut purée (sweetened)

50 g (2 oz) chocolate drops

cocoa powder, for dusting

holly leaves to decorate

1 Preheat the oven to Gas Mark 6/electric 200°C/fan oven 180°C. Line a 33 x 23 cm (13 x 9 inch) Swiss roll tin with baking parchment.

2 Place the eggs and 115 g (4 oz) sugar in a large bowl and set it over a pan of hot water. Whisk them together until the mixture is thick and creamy and leaves a trail when the whisks are lifted. Remove from the heat and whisk for another minute.

3 Sift the flour and cocoa together into the egg mixture and fold in gently with a metal spoon using a figure of eight action.

4 Spoon the mixture into the prepared tin and spread gently into the corners. Bake in the oven for about 15 minutes until it is firm to the touch and coming away from the sides of the tin.

5 Remove from the oven, place on a wire rack and cover this with a damp tea towel. Set aside until it is completely cold.

6 While it is cooling, make the ganache and then the filling. For the ganache, place half the cream and the chocolate pieces into a saucepan and melt over a gentle heat. Remove from the heat and stir to blend evenly. Set aside to cool and thicken.

7 To make the filling, whisk the remaining cream until it forms soft peaks. Place the chestnut purée and remaining sugar in another bowl and beat together. Stir in the chocolate drops and then fold in the whipped cream.

8 To assemble, invert the roulade onto a large sheet of greaseproof paper dusted with caster sugar. Taking care, peel away the lining paper, starting from a corner. Spread the chestnut cream evenly over the roulade. Using the greaseproof paper to help you, roll up the cake from one long side to another and finish with the seam underneath. Cut off 6 cm (2$^1/_2$ inches) on the diagonal from each end.

9 Place the roulade (log) onto a platter (or flat tray if freezing) and then position the two cut pieces on either side of the log and at opposite ends. Spread the chocolate ganache all over the log and make marks using a palette knife to look like tree bark. Dust the log with cocoa powder and arrange some decorations such as holly leaves on top.

Freezing: Open freeze the log and then place in a freezer bag. To thaw, unwrap, place on a serving platter and then defrost overnight in the fridge.

SCC

CHRISTMAS ICE CREAM

This is a dessert for those who prefer an ice cream dessert after a fairly heavy meal. I also like to serve it with Christmas pudding as an alternative to the traditional accompaniments. I served the ice cream to a group of girlfriends at our Christmas dinner and surrounded the base with clementines. It was a big hit! **Serves 6–8** Preparation time: 20 minutes + overnight soaking + 4 hours freezing

115 g (4 oz) raisins
4 eggs, separated
115 g (4 oz) caster sugar
425 ml (¾ pint) double cream
50 g (2 oz) glace cherries, chopped
1 tablespoon icing sugar
50 g (2 oz) nibbed almonds
3 tablespoons brandy
holly leaves, to decorate

1 Soak the raisins in the brandy overnight or longer.
2 Whisk the whites in a large bowl until they are nearly stiff and then whisk in the caster sugar, a teaspoon at a time.
3 Whisk two thirds of the cream until it reaches the soft peak stage and then stir in the egg yolks Add the cream mixture to the meringue and place in the freezer for two hours.

4 Toss the cherries with the icing sugar. Remove the meringue mixture from the freezer and add the cherries and the raisins, together with the brandy and the almonds. Return to the freezer to solidify (about another two hours).
5 Lightly oil and line a 1.2 litre (2 pint) pudding basin with cling film. Spoon the ice cream into the prepared basin and freeze until solid.
6 To serve, whip the remaining cream. Invert the ice cream onto a serving plate, remove the cling film and spread the cream all over, making peaks with the knife. Decorate with the holly leaves.

 Freezing essential

N.B. This recipe contains raw eggs - pregnant women, the elderly, babies and toddlers should avoid eating raw eggs.

SCC

CHRISTMAS FRUIT COMPOTE

This dessert is ideal for those who don't want anything too heavy after a rich meal. It can be served either warm or chilled. Here it is served with Greek yoghurt and pistachio nuts, but you could serve it with a good quality real vanilla ice cream or custard. The compote is best if made at least a day in advance so that the flavours develop.

Serves 4 Preparation time: 10 minutes + cooling overnight Cooking time: 20 minutes

115 g (4 oz) each of dried, no-soak, stoned apricots, figs, prunes and pears
50 g (2 oz) raisins
2 oranges, juice only
300 ml (½ pint) water
1 cinnamon stick
seeds of 3 green cardamom pods, crushed
150 ml (¼ pint) ruby port
250 g (9 oz) Greek yoghurt
25 g (1 oz) pistachio nuts

1 Place the dried fruit in a saucepan with the juice of the oranges, 300 ml (½ pint) water, the cinnamon stick and crushed cardamom seeds. Bring to the boil, cover with a lid and simmer gently for 20 minutes.

2 Remove from the heat, remove the cinnamon and stir in the port. Allow to cool and then place in the fridge overnight.

3 If serving warm, re-heat over a gentle heat. To serve, spoon the compote into individual glass bowls, spoon some yoghurt on top and scatter pistachio nuts on top of the yoghurt.

 Freezing not recommended

Tip: To make it easier for your guests to eat, you could cut the apricots, figs, prunes and pears into bite-sized pieces.

SCC

CHRISTMAS STAR TRIFLE

I'm not a fan of Christmas pudding so each year I try to create an alternative that includes chocolate! I would like to dedicate this dessert to my friend Karen, a fellow chocoholic who loves Green and Black's Maya Gold chocolate – the inclusion of this chocolate in the custard really complements the orange in the poached cranberries. It's quick to prepare since good quality convenience products are used. **Serves 6–8**
Preparation time: 45 minutes

3 standard size, chocolate muffins
4 tablespoons cranberry sauce
115 g (4 oz) fresh cranberries
3 tablespoons fresh orange juice
190 g (6½ oz) caster sugar
500 g carton of custard
115 g (4 oz) Green and Black's
   Maya Gold chocolate, broken
   into pieces
150 ml (¼ pint) ruby Port
juice of 1 lemon
225 ml (8 fl oz) double cream
To decorate
a home made Christmas star made
   from melted chocolate
cocoa

1 Slice each muffin into three and spread each slice with cranberry sauce. Arrange in the base of a glass trifle bowl.

2 Place the cranberries, orange juice, 3 tablespoons water and 115 g (4 oz) of the caster sugar in a saucepan, bring to the boil and simmer gently until the cranberries are cooked.

3 Strain the cranberries, reserving the poaching liquid, and spoon over the muffins. Sprinkle 3 tablespoons of the reserved liquid over the cranberries and muffins.

4 Empty the custard into a saucepan and heat very gently until it is on the point of boiling. Remove from the heat, add the chocolate pieces and stir until the chocolate has melted. Pour over the cranberries and chill while you prepare the syllabub.

5 Place the port, lemon juice and remaining sugar in a large bowl and stir until the sugar has dissolved. Add the cream and whisk, starting on a low speed to begin with, until the mixture has begun to thicken. Pour over the chocolate custard.

6 To decorate, either use a chocolate star cut out about seven stars from a sheet of paper and arrange lightly on the syllabub. Sieve cocoa powder all over the surface and carefully lift the pieces of paper form the top. Alternatively, you could simply dust the surface with sieved cocoa powder.

Freezing not recommended

SCC

AROMATHERAPY BAG

An aromatherapy bag can be warmed in the microwave to give pain relief for muscle cramps, stiff joints or backache. To use your aromatherapy bag, put it in the microwave with a glass of water (to stop the rice drying out) on HIGH for $1\frac{1}{2}$–2 minutes. You will have to judge the temperature you want, but take care not to overheat the bag. Alternatively, if you want to use your bag like an ice pack (which doesn't also allow you to enjoy the scent), simply freeze it for 1 hour before use.

You will need:
- cotton, brushed cotton
- 350 g (12 oz) long grain white rice
- dried rosemary, lavender, essential oil
- ribbon (optional)

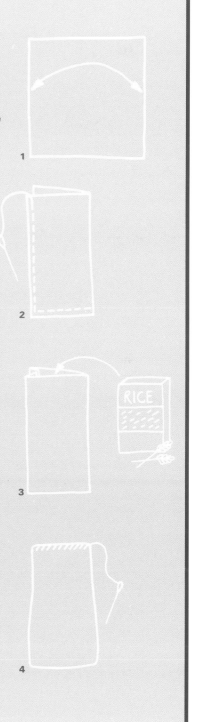

1 First, make a pouch for the rice by cutting a square of pure cotton, (man-made fabrics will melt in the microwave) approximately 25 cm (10 inches) square.

2 Fold it in half, with the right side on the inside, and sew together along both long edges and one short edge. Turn it through and you have a small pouch in which to put the rice.

3 Fill the bag with about 350 g (12 oz) of uncooked long grain white rice and some potpourri of dried rosemary, lavender and a few drops of your favourite essential oil. Do not use any alternatives to long grain white rice.

4 Turn in the open end and sew it together so that the rice is sealed in the bag.

5 Make a cover for your rice pouch out of a fabric of your choice. This should also be made of cotton. Brushed cotton will give you a lovely soft bag.

6 Cut a piece of fabric slightly larger than the piece for the rice pouch, say 26 cm x 29 cm ($10\frac{1}{4}$ inches x $11\frac{1}{2}$ inches), and fold it along the shorter edge. Join together, leaving one of the short ends open so that you can insert and remove the rice pouch. Finish the cover like a pillowcase or add a ribbon tie. To clean, wash the cover, not the rice pouch.

Christmas
Day

The big day has arrived! Whether you are having a large number or a small family gathering, we have created some delicious recipes for you to prepare. There is traditional turkey as well as a recipe for a boned turkey if you have limited oven space or simply want a smaller bird to cook, a delicious chicken recipe, and a goose recipe for those who want a change from turkey.

All the traditional vegetables are included but they have been given a make-over to make them irresistible – even people who claim not to like sprouts will hopefully change their minds after trying the Creamed Brussels Sprouts with Chestnuts. Many of these recipes can be prepared in advance, which relieves the pressure on such a hectic day.

Many people say that one of the most difficult things about entertaining is timing – getting all the dishes ready at the right time. With this in mind, we have created a timetable for your Christmas lunch, which we hope you will find useful. Whichever recipes you choose, have a delicious meal and a wonderful time.

Roast Goose with Thickened Gravy *(page 62)*

BUTTERED ROAST TURKEY WITH CHESTNUT STUFFING

For most people Christmas would not be Christmas without a turkey and all the trimmings so tuck into this classic recipe for the perfect Christmas lunch.

Serves 8 with plenty of leftovers
Preparation time: 30 minutes + 30 minutes resting Cooking time: 3½–4 hours

1 oven-ready, free-range or bronze turkey, 4.5–5.5 kg (10–12 lb)
2 onions, quartered
1 lemon, quartered
175 g (6 oz) slightly salted butter,
225 g (8 oz) streaky bacon
salt and freshly ground black pepper
Chestnut Stuffing (see page 48)

1 Remove the neck and giblets from inside the turkey.

2 Sit the neck end on a board and generously season the inside of the cavity with salt and pepper. Put in the onions and lemon.

3 Place the bird breast side up, lift the neck flap and remove the wishbone to make carving easier. Gently work the skin away from the breasts by easing your hand gently under the skin of the breast. Put some of the butter under the skin.

4 Spoon the Chestnut Stuffing into the neck cavity, but do not pack too tightly. Cover with the neck flap and fold it into the back of the bird. With the bird breast side up, fold the wing tips under the body, catching in the neck skin.

5 Re-weigh the bird and calculate the cooking time. Allow 20 minutes per 450 g (1 lb) plus 20 minutes. Place in a large roasting tin. Smear the skin all over with butter and season with salt and pepper. Cover the breast with the rashers of streaky bacon.

6 Cover the bird with foil and roast for the calculated time at a temperature of Gas Mark 4/ electric oven 180°C/fan oven 160°C, basting it every hour.

7 To test if cooked, insert a metal skewer into the thigh at the thickest part; if it is cooked, the juices should run clear.

8 Leave the turkey to rest for 30 minutes, still covered in foil, before carving.

9 Serve with gravy, Cranberry Kumquat Sauce (page 46), and Bacon and Chipolata Rolls (page 65).

 Freezing not recommended

Tip: Get the turkey ready for roasting on Christmas Eve to enjoy a more leisurely start to the day. Do try to buy a fresh bird, preferably from a local farmer, but it is advisable to order well in advance to be sure of getting the size you want. Also, check your oven size to make sure the turkey will fit.

MEW

BONED TURKEY ROLL WITH DATE, ORANGE & ALMOND STUFFING

This is a good way to cook turkey, particularly if oven space is limited. Get your butcher to bone the turkey for you or alternatively you can use a ready prepared boneless breast joint or turkey crown. The use of a packet stuffing mix saves time and the only fiddly bit is tying up the roll. Any left over makes an excellent cold cut, which can be served with salads. **Serves 8**
Preparation time: 40 minutes
Cooking time: 3 hours

**1 oven-ready boned turkey,
    approximately 3.4 kg (7 lb 8 oz)**
For the stuffing:
1 tablespoon vegetable oil
1 onion, chopped finely
2 garlic cloves, crushed
100 g (3½ oz) bacon, diced finely
300 g (10 oz) pork fillet, minced
**1 packet of date, orange and
    almond stuffing mix**
50 g (2 oz) butter, slightly softened
**salt and freshly ground black
    pepper**

For the glaze:
125 ml (4½ fl oz) orange juice
1 tablespoon soft brown sugar
2 teaspoons Dijon mustard

1 Prepare the stuffing as instructed on the packet.
2 Heat the oil and then lightly fry the onion, garlic and bacon in the oil.
3 Mince the pork in a food processor.
4 Mix the date, orange and almond stuffing ingredients together and season generously with salt and pepper. To check if the seasoning is correct, fry a little bit of the mixture and taste.
5 Place the turkey skin-side down and place the stuffing down the middle. Tuck in the ends over the filling and draw the long sides of the bird over the stuffing. Using a trussing needle and fine string, sew the edges together. Tie the roll again at intervals along the bird to get a good shape, but do not tie too tightly or it will burst during cooking.
6 Weigh the bird and place breast side up in a roasting tin. Smear all over with the softened butter and season with salt and pepper. Cover with foil to make a parcel and roast at Gas Mark 4/electric oven 180°C/fan oven 160°C for 15 minutes per 450 g (1 lb). Baste frequently.

7 Mix the glaze ingredients together.
8 For the last 30 minutes remove the foil, brush the turkey roll with the glaze and raise the temperature to Gas Mark 6/electric oven 200°C/fan oven 180°C to brown.
9 Test with a fine skewer and if the juices run clear, the turkey is cooked. Leave to rest for 15 minutes and remove the string before carving.

 Freezing not recommended

Alternatively, for a very quick glaze, you can simply use a fine-shred or jelly orange marmalade.

MEW

ROAST GOOSE WITH THICKENED GRAVY

The goose was always England's festive bird, valued not only for its rich meat and fat but also for the down and feathers. It was traditionally served on Michaelmas day, the 29th of September, with apples (at a time when there would have been plenty of windfalls). A goose is an ideal choice if you fancy a change from turkey for Christmas lunch. **Serves 6**
Preparation time: 30 minutes + 20 minutes resting Cooking time: 2½–3 hours

1 oven-ready fresh or frozen goose 4.5 kg (10 lb)
1 onion, chopped roughly
10 sage leaves or 1 teaspoon dried sage
Sage, Onion and Pickled Walnut Stuffing (see page 45)
salt and freshly ground black pepper
fresh sage leaves, to garnish
To serve
Stuffed Apples (see page 69)
Roast Potatoes (see page 72)
Braised Red Cabbage (see page 78)
Thickened Gravy (opposite) (see Tip)

1 Remove the giblets and use them to make the stock for the gravy (use the same recipe as for the turkey stock). Cut off the large pieces of fat from inside the bird's cavity. Rinse inside and out and pat the skin dry with kitchen towel. Season the inside of the body cavity with salt and pepper and put in the onion and fresh or dried sage (these are just to add flavour while cooking).

2 Stuff the neck end of the bird with the Sage, Onion and Pickled Walnut Stuffing. Press it in as far as it will go and then pull the neck flap back over the neck and underneath. Hold the flap in place by sewing with a trussing needle and fine string or use a small metal skewer.

3 Preheat the oven to Gas Mark 6/electric oven 200°C/fan oven 180°C. Re-weigh the bird and calculate the cooking time. Allow 15 minutes per 450 g (1 lb) plus 15 minutes.

4 Rub the goose with salt and prick the skin all over, using a fine metal skewer. Try not to pierce the flesh. Lay the goose on a rack or trivet in a roasting tin, breast side down, and place in the oven for 30 minutes.

5 Reduce the oven temperature to Gas Mark 3/electric oven 160°C/fan oven 140°C and continue roasting, basting frequently. Every 30–40 minutes, pour off the fat from the roasting tin (see Tip below). For the last 30 minutes, raise the oven temperature again to Gas Mark 6/electric oven 200°C/fan oven 180°C and turn the bird breast side up (use oven gloves or a thick cloth). When the skin is golden and crisp, cover the goose with foil to prevent further browning. While the goose is cooking, make the gravy (opposite).

6 To test if done, insert a metal skewer into the thigh at the thickest part; if it is cooked, the juices should run clear. If they are still pink, cook for little longer

7 When the goose is cooked, leave it to rest on a warm serving platter, covered with foil, for 20 minutes.

8 To serve, remove the trussing string or metal skewer and carve the goose. Scoop out the Sage,

Onion and Pickled Walnut Stuffing and serve with Stuffed Apples, Roast Potatoes and Braised Red Cabbage, adding thickened gravy to taste (see recipe opposite). Garnish with fresh sage.

 Freezing not recommended

Tip: If the bird is frozen, remove it from the bag and place it on a tray to catch the drips, in the lowest part of the refrigerator until it is completely thawed. As a guide, allow 17 hours thawing per kg, so this may take up to three days for a 4.5 kg bird. The easiest way to remove excess fat is to take the roasting tin from the oven and lift the goose, still on its rack, on to a baking sheet, then pour the fat into an oven proof basin. Replace the bird and rack in the roasting tin and return to the oven to continue cooking. Use the goose fat to roast the potatoes.

MEW

THICKENED GRAVY

Serves 6 Preparation and cooking time: 30 minutes

2 tablespoons goose fat from the roasting tin
1 small onion, chopped finely
1 celery stick, chopped finely
1 small carrot, chopped finely
25 g (1oz) plain flour
600 ml (1 pint) giblet stock
200 g (7 oz) can of chopped tomatoes
1 bouquet garni (parsley stalks, bay leaves and thyme)
150 ml (¼ pint) red wine
salt and freshly ground black pepper

1 While the goose is cooking, make the gravy. Use 2 tablespoons of the goose fat from the roasting tin and put it in a pan. Add the onion, celery and carrot and cook until soft.
2 Add the flour and continue cooking until the roux turns a brown colour. Add the giblet stock, tomatoes, bouquet garni, salt and pepper and bring to the boil. Simmer for 10 minutes.
3 Strain the gravy through a sieve into a clean pan. Add the wine and heat through. Season to taste. Serve the gravy in a warm gravy boat.

 Freezing not recommended

MEW

BRETON STYLE CHICKEN SUPRÊME WITH CALVADOS

Chicken is an inexpensive choice for the Christmas meal but cooking it in the cider and Calvados makes it taste special, particularly if you choose to buy a bird from the organic or outdoor reared range. **Serves 6**
Preparation time: 45 minutes
Cooking time: 40 minutes

225 g (8 oz) prepared vegetables:
  2 leeks, green part only, sliced finely
  1 carrot, cut into matchsticks
  1 large celery stick, sliced finely
6 skinless chicken suprêmes or breast fillets
25 g (1 oz) plain flour, seasoned with salt and pepper
1 tablespoon vegetable oil
50 g (2 oz) butter
300 ml (½ pint) vintage dry cider
150 ml (¼ pint) light crème fraîche (half-fat)
1 tablespoon Calvados (apple brandy)
salt and freshly ground black pepper

For the vegetable garnish
1 carrot, cut into matchsticks
2 leeks, white part only, sliced finely
125 g (4½ oz) baby button mushrooms
25 g (1 oz) butter

1 First prepare the vegetables. Wash the leek thoroughly, remove the root and cut away the dark green end of the stalk. Cut in half down the middle. Cut each length of leek in half along its length. Put the flat edge on a chopping board and finely slice across. Remember to separate green and white parts. The white part is used later as a vegetable garnish. Peel and cut the carrot into 5 cm (2 inch) lengths. Cut the lengths into thin slices and the slices into thin strips. They should look like matchsticks. Cut the celery across the stalk, into finely sliced pieces.

2 Coat the chicken in seasoned flour.

3 Melt the oil and 25 g (1 oz) of the butter in a frying pan and cook gently on both sides (approximately 6–8 minutes). Try not to let it discolour. Remove the chicken and place it in a shallow ovenproof dish, then keep it warm.

4 Add the remaining butter to the pan, add the prepared vegetables and cook for 3–4 minutes until they begin to soften.

5 Pour in the cider and bring to the boil, stirring all the time. Remove from the heat and stir in the crème fraîche.

6 Pour over the chicken and cook, covered, for approximately 40 minutes until the chicken is tender.

7 Approximately 15 minutes before serving, cook the vegetable garnish. Melt 25 g (1 oz) of butter in a pan and add the vegetables. Cook slowly with the lid on the pan until they are just cooked.

8 When the chicken is cooked, add the Calvados (brandy) and stir in. Taste and adjust the seasoning.

9 Spoon the cooked vegetable garnish down the centre of the dish and serve.

Freezing recommended – freeze when dish is cooked at the end of stage 6 and freeze the vegetable garnish separately.

MEW

BACON & CHIPOLATA ROLLS

This recipe combines bacon rolls and chipolatas and saves space in the oven when it is at a premium. **Makes 12** Preparation time: 15 minutes Cooking time: 25–30 minutes cooking

6 rashers of streaky bacon

12 chipolata sausages

1 Remove the rind from the bacon rashers using a pair of scissors.

2 Lay the rashers on a chopping board and, with the back of a cook's knife, smooth and stretch each rasher. Cut each one in half.

3 Wrap a piece of bacon around each chipolata and thread them on to a skewer.

4 Put the rolls on a baking tray and bake at Gas Mark 4/electric oven 180°C/fan oven 160°C for 25–30 minutes or until thoroughly cooked. Alternatively, cook them under the grill for 10–15 minutes until thoroughly cooked.

Freezing: Pack the rolls into containers at the end of step 3, then seal and freeze them. Thaw in a refrigerator.

MEW

POPCORN AND CRANBERRY GARLANDS

These garlands will only last a few days before the berries become soft. When it is past its best, take down the garland and hang it in the garden as a Christmas treat for the birds. The quantities will depend on the length of garland you are making.

You will need:

- 1 metre (3 feet) string
- needle
- fresh cranberries
- popped popcorn (stale popcorn works best with no added salt or butter).

1 Take about a 1 metre length of string and tie a knot about 12 cm (4½ inches) from one end.

2 Thread a needle onto the other end and begin stringing the cranberries and popcorn alternately.

3 Push them together as tightly as possible because the cranberries shrink.

Tip: If you want a longer garland, tie lengths together and cover the knots in the string with ribbons. For smaller garlands, use wire instead of string and wind them around wreaths or the base of candles. Do not place the garland on light surfaces or fabrics as the cranberries will stain.

AG

SOLE, PRAWN & SPINACH ROULADES AU GRATIN WITH HOLLANDAISE SAUCE

Sole rolled in this way looks particularly elegant and can be served either as a delightful and tasty main course or as the fish course in a full Christmas menu.

Serves 6 Preparation time: 50 minutes Cooking time: 20 minutes

12 lemon sole fillets, skinned

12 spinach leaves, washed

150 g (5 oz) prawns, liquidised with a little butter

butter, to grease the dish

8 peppercorns

1 slice of onion

1 bay leaf

100 ml (3½ fl oz) white wine

100 ml (3½ fl oz) water

salt and freshly ground black pepper

For the hollandaise sauce

2 egg yolks

1½ tablespoons lemon juice

75 g (2¾ oz) unsalted butter

salt and freshly ground pepper

For the white wine sauce

25 g (1 oz) butter

1 tablespoon plain flour

5 tablespoons single cream

salt and freshly ground black pepper

To serve:

slices of lemon

a few sprigs of fresh dill

1 Preheat the oven to Gas Mark 4/ electric oven 180°C/fan oven 160°C.

2 Wash and dry the fillets and place them, skinned side up, on the work surface. Season with salt and pepper. Lay the spinach and the prawns on top of each fillet, roll each one up and secure with a cocktail stick.

3 Grease an ovenproof dish and place the roulades in. Add the peppercorns, onion, bay leaf, wine and water. Cover and poach in the oven for 15–20 minutes (or see Tip).

4 Meanwhile make the Hollandaise sauce (see recipe, above right).

5 Remove the roulades from the liquid using a slotted spoon, put them in a serving dish and keep warm. Remove the cocktail sticks.

6 Strain the liquid and measure out 200 ml (7 fl oz fish stock).

7 Make the white wine sauce by melting the butter in a saucepan, adding the flour and cooking to make a roux for 1–2 minutes. Gradually add 200 ml (7 fl oz) fish stock and stir until thickened. Add the cream and simmer for 2–3 minutes.

8 Pour the white wine sauce over the roulades.

9 Spoon a tablespoon of Hollandaise sauce on each roulade and brown under the grill.

10 Serve with slices or wedges of lemon. Allow two roulades per person for a main course or one roulade each for a fish course.

Hollandaise sauce

1 Put the egg yolks, lemon juice and seasoning into a liquidiser goblet and run the machine until the ingredients are well blended.

2 Heat the butter in a small saucepan until just foaming. Do not brown.

3 Pour half the butter into the liquidiser and run for a few seconds until the mixture is well blended.

4 Pour in the remaining butter and run the machine until the sauce thickens and turns a creamy yellow.

Tip: The roulades can be poached using a microwave cooker and will take only 4–5 minutes.

MEW

HANDMADE NOTEBOOK

What nicer gift than a handmade book? You could fill it with photos to make it special.

If this is the first book you've made, try something small. These instructions are for a square book measuring 10 x 10 cm (4 x 4 inches).

You will need:
- 2 pieces 10 x 10 cm (4 x 4 inches) strawboard or mounting board for the covers
- 10 x 1 cm (4 x 1/2 inch) strawboard or mounting board for the spine
- 14 x 4 cm (5 1/2 x 1 1/2 inches) fabric (or paper) to cover the spine
- 2 pieces 12 x 12 cm (4 1/2 x 4 1/2 inches) fabric (or paper) to cover the front and back covers
- 12 sheets 18 x 9 cm (7 x 3 1/2 inches) paper for the pages and endpaper
- 18 x 9 cm (7 x 3 1/2 inches) coloured paper for the flysheet
- PVA glue
- stanley knife
- needle
- strong thread

1 Apply a thin layer of glue to the fabric (or paper) for the spine, place the strawboard spine in the middle. Place the covers on either side of the spine, leaving a gap of just less than 5 cm (2 inches) between the pieces to allow for the fold. Fold the top and bottom of the spine fabric (or paper) over the board and put aside to dry.

2 Fold the pages widthways and place one folded page on top of the other. Fold the flysheet around the outside. Make 5 holes down the centre: one 1 cm (1/2 inch) from the top, another 1 cm (1/2 inch) from the bottom, another in the centre. Make one on either side of the central hole. Pull the thread through the central hole, out at the top, back in at the centre and out at the bottom. Knot the ends at the centre.

3 Apply a thin layer of glue to the fabric (or paper) for the front cover. Lay the front portion of the cover on to the paper so that it just overlaps the fabric on the spine. Cut the cover diagonally at each corner, fold over and glue. Repeat this for the back cover.

4 To complete the book, glue the flysheet to the covers and spine, leaving a small margin around the outside.

STUFFED APPLES

This is a great alternative to traditional apple sauce. **Serves 6–8** Preparation time: 10 minutes Cooking time: 25 minutes

6–8 small dessert apples

12–16 ready to eat prunes

50 g (2 oz) butter

50 g (2 oz) demerara sugar

6–8 teaspoons quince or redcurrant jelly

1 Wash the apples, remove the cores and score with a sharp knife around the circumferences. Stand the cored apples in a baking dish.

2 Cream the butter and sugar together and mix in the prunes.

3 Refill the apple cores and top each one with a teaspoon of jelly.

4 Bake for 25 minutes at Gas Mark 4/electric oven 180°C/fan oven 160°C.

Freezing not recommended

TURKEY GRAVY

The best turkey gravy is made from the giblets and it's worth making a stock beforehand and storing it in the refrigerator until needed. **Serves 8** Preparation time for the stock: 10 minutes + cooling Cooking time for the stock: 45 minutes Preparation and cooking time for the gravy: 20 minutes

For the turkey stock

turkey giblets

1 onion, sliced thickly

1 carrot, chopped thickly

1 celery stick, chopped

1 leek, green part only, chopped

2–3 bay leaves

6–8 peppercorns

1.2 litres (2 pints) water

For the gravy

pan juices

2 tablespoons plain flour

600 ml (1 pint) turkey stock

2 tablespoons redcurrant jelly

salt and freshly ground black pepper

1 Make the stock well in advance. Put all the ingredients in a large pan and bring to the boil.

2 Remove any scum that floats to the surface and then simmer for about 45 minutes.

3 Strain, cool and keep refrigerated until required.

4 Make the gravy while the turkey is resting. Drain off as much of the fat in the roasting tin as possible, leaving the dark brown juices behind.

5 Heat the roasting pan on the hob and add the flour to the pan juices, stirring to make a smooth paste.

6 Cook for 1–2 minutes until it turns a rich, brown colour and then gradually whisk in the stock. Bring to the boil and when it has thickened, add the fruit jelly and simmer for 5 minutes. Season to taste.

7 Serve in a warm sauceboat. If you prefer a richer gravy substitute red wine for 150 ml (¼ pint) stock or add some sherry with the fruit jelly.

 Freezing not recommended

MEW

CHRISTMAS WALDORF SALAD WITH GRILLED GOAT'S CHEESE

This salad is a perfect beginning to the Christmas meal – it is light, colourful and most of it can be prepared in advance. It has the traditional ingredients of a Waldorf Salad but, instead of the dressing being a rich mayonnaise, it is a light cranberry and apple one. **Serves 6**
Preparation and cooking time: 20 minutes

For the dressing

4 tablespoons cranberry sauce

3 tablespoons extra virgin olive oil

6 tablespoons apple juice

2 tablespoons red wine vinegar

1 teaspoon wholegrain mustard

**salt and freshly ground black
  pepper**

For the salad

4 red dessert apples

**4 celery sticks, plus leaves to
  garnish**

50 g (2 oz) walnut pieces

3 x 70 g logs of goat's cheese

a packet rocket salad leaves

1 To make the dressing, simply place all the ingredients in a large bowl and blend with a small whisk. Transfer half the dressing to another bowl.

2 Cut the apples and celery sticks into small pieces. Place them in one of the bowls with the dressing and toss together so that all the pieces are coated.

3 Preheat the grill to a high setting. Cut each log in half and place, cut side up, under the grill. Grill the cheeses until they melt and are golden brown.

4 While they are cooking, toss the salad leaves in the remaining dressing and arrange on the serving plates. Pile the apples and celery in the centre of the salad leaves and scatter the walnut pieces on top.

5 Place each cheese half on top, or you could arrange in slices, and serve immediately.

 Freezing not recommended

SCC

ROAST POTATOES

Who can resist perfect roast potatoes? I use the word 'perfect' since badly cooked roast potatoes are not a joy to eat. They should be crisp and golden on the outside and fluffy on the inside. If you follow the method below, I promise you will have wonderful 'roasties' every time. This year, my husband, Terry, devoted a whole allotment to growing potatoes so I've had plenty of practice!

Serves 6 Preparation time: 20 minutes Cooking time: 1 hour

1 kg (2 lb) potatoes (Maris Piper and King Edward are best), peeled
2 tablespoons sunflower oil
1 teaspoon English Mustard powder
sea salt and freshly ground black pepper

1 Preheat the oven to Gas Mark 5/electric 190°C/fan oven 170°C.
2 Cut the potatoes into evenly sized pieces. Place in a saucepan, cover with cold water, bring to the boil and simmer for 5 minutes.
3 While the potatoes are cooking, pour the oil into a large roasting tin and place in the oven so that the tin and oil get hot.
4 Drain the potatoes well and return them to the saucepan. Cover with the lid and give them a good shake – this will roughen the edges of the potato and make the skins really crisp.
5 Remove the tin from the oven and tip in the potatoes – they should sizzle in the hot fat. Roll them around so that they are all coated in the fat. Sprinkle the mustard powder over the potatoes, then the salt and pepper.
6 Roast in the oven for about an hour until they are crisp and golden brown in colour.

 Freezing not recommended

SCC

CREAMED BRUSSELS SPROUTS WITH CHESTNUTS

I have to be honest and admit that I am not a huge fan of sprouts, but I love them prepared in this way. The addition of the chopped chestnuts makes them more interesting. They can also be prepared in advance, which is a great help, and then simply reheated in the microwave.
Serves 6 Preparation time: 15 minutes Cooking time: 10 minutes

675 g (1 lb 8 oz) brussels sprouts
200 ml (7 fl oz) single cream
salt and freshly ground black pepper
100 g (3½ oz) cooked and peeled chestnuts, chopped roughly

1 Trim the sprouts and remove the outer leaves, as necessary. Place in a saucepan and add just enough boiling water to cover them. Add a little salt. Simmer for about 10 minutes until the sprouts are tender.
2 Drain them and place them in a food processor or blender. Blend to a purée and then add the cream in a steady stream, with the motor still running. Blend to a smooth purée.
3 Season to taste with salt and freshly ground black pepper. Fold in the chopped chestnuts and spoon into the serving dish.

❄ *Freezing: When cool, transfer the sprout purée to a plastic tub and cover with a lid. To thaw, place the tub in the fridge and thaw overnight. Transfer the sprout purée to a serving dish and reheat in the microwave, ideally, as the oven will dry the purée a little.*

SCC

BAKED MUSTARD & ORANGE CARROTS

This is a lovely and flavoursome way of serving carrots. The mustard isn't obvious but compliments the orange. When you unwrap the parcel, the aroma is wonderful. The parcel can be prepared in advance and then popped into the oven when you are ready to cook the carrots. **Serves 6** Preparation time: 10 minutes Cooking time: 30 minutes

675 g (1½ lb) carrots, peeled
6 tablespoons freshly squeezed orange juice
25 g (1 oz) butter
1 tablespoon wholegrain mustard
salt and freshly ground black pepper

1 Preheat the oven to Gas Mark 6/electric 200°C/fan oven 180°C.

2 Cut a large, long piece of foil and fold it in half.

3 Cut the carrots into fairly thin sticks about 8 cm (3 inches) long. Place them in a mixing bowl and pour over the orange juice. Add the mustard and salt and pepper. Mix well so that the carrots are coated evenly.

4 Spoon the carrots and their juices into the middle of the foil. Dot the butter over the top. Bring the edges of the foil together and scrunch them up, making sure that there are no gaps.

5 Bake the parcel on a baking sheet in the oven for 30 minutes. You may need to cook it for a few more minutes depending on how thick your carrot sticks are.

 *Freezing not recommended*

SCC

PARSNIP DAUPHINOISE

I adore *pommes dauphinoise* and thought that making a similar dish using parsnips would make an interesting alternative to roast parsnips. The advantage is that it can be prepared in advance and then popped in the oven with the roast potatoes and other accompaniments. **Serves 6**
Preparation time: 20 minutes
Cooking time: 30 minutes

800 g (1 lb 12 oz) parsnips, peeled
200 ml tub of crème fraîche
50 g (2 oz) freshly grated Parmesan
  cheese
freshly grated nutmeg
salt and freshly ground black
  pepper

1 Preheat the oven to Gas Mark 5/electric 190°C/fan oven 170°C. Butter a shallow gratin dish.

2 Cover the parsnips with cold, salted water and bring them to the boil. Simmer for 5 minutes until they are just tender.

3 Drain and then arrange the slices in the prepared dish. Season the parsnips with the nutmeg, salt and pepper and spread the crème fraîche over them.

4 Sprinkle the grated Parmesan on top and then bake in the oven for 30 minutes until the topping is crisp and golden.

Freezing not recommended

Tip: To make it easier to spread the crème fraîche evenly over the parsnips, warm it a little – this is easily done in the microwave.

SCC

CHEESY POTATO BAKES

These little bakes are real comfort food, full of flavour. They can be prepared in advance and simply reheated, which is great for Christmas Day – the less you have to cook on the day, the better! If you prepare them in advance, remove them from the dishes when cold and place them on a greased baking sheet. **Makes 8**
Preparation time: 30 minutes
Cooking time: 15–20 minutes

**900 g (2 lb) potatoes, peeled and
cut into evenly sized pieces
150 g packet of cream cheese with
garlic and herbs e.g. Boursin
2 eggs, lightly beaten
salt and freshly ground black
pepper
50 g (2 oz) Gruyère cheese, grated**

1 Preheat the oven to Gas Mark 6/electric 200°C/fan oven 180°C. Grease and base-line eight ramekin dishes.
2 Boil the potatoes until they are tender. Drain them well and mash.
3 Stir in the cream cheese and eggs and mix until they have been incorporated. Season with salt and pepper.
4 Divide between the dishes, level the surfaces and sprinkle with the grated cheese.
5 Bake in the oven for 15–20 minutes until cooked through and the cheese is golden brown. Run a knife around the ramekins, tip each bake onto the palm of your hand and place on the serving dish – you may need to protect your hands if you don't have cook's hands!

 *Freezing not recommended*

Tip: Whenever I need to line the bases of ramekin dishes, I use the little waxed discs normally used for placing on top of preserves!

SCC

GIFT BOW

You will need:

- 10 cm (4 inch) long and 2 cm (¾ inch) wide satin ribbon
- scissors.
- A friend's hands would make life easier for the first few attempts!
- a small decoration to add to the centre of the ribbon, such as tiny pinecones, baubles, or you could run your scissors up some narrow strips of ribbon to make curls

1 Cut a piece of ribbon about 10 cm (4 inches) long and tear it lengthwise to get a narrow strip. This will be used to tie the bow.

2 Wind the ribbon seven or eight times around your hand to form the loops. You could cut a card template (to wind the ribbon around) if you want bigger or smaller loops. Don't wind too tightly or you won't be able to get the ribbon off the card.

3 Hold all the loops together and cut two small "v" shapes from the centre of the ribbon like this ><. Use the narrow strip of ribbon to tie the bow here as tightly as possible. You could add a staple first if you want to make it even more secure.

4 To spread the loops around, take alternate loops and carefully fold and twist them, one forwards and clockwise, the next back and anti-clockwise until they form a bow.

5 Trim the ends of the loops and the narrow strip so they don't show and, if you like, add a tiny decoration in the centre of your bow – this will also help to hide any mistakes in the centre. If the narrow strip is long enough, you could tie it around your gift. Otherwise, stick it down with double-sided tape or glue it in place.

AG

BRAISED RED CABBAGE WITH APPLE

This is such a versatile vegetable dish to serve at Christmas time – it can be prepared in advance and reheated. It freezes well and is delicious both hot and cold. What more could one want? Serves 6 Preparation time: 20 minutes Cooking time: 2 hours

675 g (1½ lb) red cabbage, quartered, thick stalk removed and shredded

1 onion, peeled, halved and sliced thinly

1 large cooking apple, peeled, cored and sliced

½ teaspoon ground coriander

½ teaspoon cinnamon

½ teaspoon nutmeg

2 tablespoons light muscovado sugar

5 tablespoons red wine vinegar

large knob of butter

salt and freshly ground black pepper

2 tablespoons redcurrant jelly

1 Preheat the oven to Gas Mark 2/electric 150°C/fan oven 130°C.

2 Arrange half the cabbage in a layer in a fairly large casserole dish, followed by half the onion, apple and sugar. Season with half the spices and salt and pepper. Repeat the layers, pour over the red wine vinegar and dot the surface with the butter.

3 Cover the casserole with a tight-fitting lid and bake in the oven for about 2 hours, stirring a couple of times during cooking. When cooked, stir in the redcurrant jelly and serve.

Freezing: Allow the braised cabbage to cool and then transfer to a plastic tub, cover with a lid and freeze. To thaw, thaw at room temperature, transfer to a serving dish and then reheat, either in the oven or in a microwave oven.

SCC

CELERIAC PURÉE WITH ONIONS & MUSTARD SEEDS

Celeriac is a very underrated vegetable. It has a mild celery flavour which accompanies most highly flavoured dishes beautifully. Celeriac purées to a lovely creamy texture. The fried onion and mustard seed topping adds an interesting flavour and texture. As with the creamed sprouts, this can be prepared in advance and simply reheated.

Serves 6 Preparation time: 15 minutes Cooking time: 15–20 minutes

900 g (2 lb) celeriac, peeled and cut into chunks
25 g (1 oz) butter
2 tablespoons single cream
1 tablespoon olive oil
1 onion, sliced thinly
2 teaspoons mustard seeds
salt and freshly ground black pepper

1 Place the celeriac in a saucepan and add sufficient boiling water to cover. Season with salt. Simmer for 15–20 minutes until tender.

2 Drain well and either mash or blend in a food processor with the butter. Add the cream and seasoning. Transfer to a serving dish and keep warm.

3 Heat the olive oil in a frying pan and fry the onion quickly, stirring often, until browned. Add the mustard seeds and fry until they begin to make a popping noise. Spoon the mixture over the celeriac.

Tip: If you're not cooking the celeriac immediately, add some lemon juice to the water to prevent it from discolouring.

SCC

FLORENTINES

These little chocolate-coated biscuits make a lovely present for serving with coffee, either in the morning or after dinner. The addition of the stem ginger gives them a bit of a 'kick'.

Makes about 20–24 Preparation and cooking times: 40 minutes + cooling + setting

50 g (2 oz) butter

50 g (2 oz) demerara sugar

50 g (2 oz) golden syrup

50 g (2 oz) plain flour

25 g (1 oz) flaked almonds

25 g (1 oz) walnut pieces

25 g (1 oz) glacé cherries, chopped finely

25 g (1 oz) stem ginger, chopped finely

80 g (3 oz) white chocolate, melted

80 g (3 oz) plain chocolate, melted

1 Preheat the oven to Gas Mark 4/electric 180°C/fan oven 160°C.

2 Cut out baking parchment paper to fit two large baking sheets.

3 Place the butter, sugar and syrup in a saucepan and heat gently, stirring occasionally, until the butter has melted.

4 Remove from the heat and add the remaining ingredients, except the white and plain chocolate, mixing thoroughly.

5 Spoon small amounts of the mixture onto the baking sheets, leaving plenty of space for them to spread. Try to ensure that you have at least one piece of cherry in each biscuit.

6 Bake in the oven for 8–10 minutes until they are golden brown. At this point the edges will be lacy and the shapes of some will probably be a bit untidy. If you want neat circles, now is the time to tidy the edges using a small palette knife.

7 Allow the florentines to cool and then carefully lift them off the parchment paper onto the cooling rack with the same side facing upwards.

8 When they have cooled completely cooled, turn the florentines over on the cooling rack and spread half of them with white chocolate and the other half with the plain chocolate. Using a fork, make a zigzag pattern on the chocolate.

9 Leave to set and then store in an airtight tin.

SCC

CHRISTMAS DAY TIMETABLE

Detailed below is a timetable for Christmas Day, which has been prepared on the assumption that lunch will be served at 2.00 pm (if you plan to eat at a different time, simply alter the times accordingly). If you are fortunate enough to have a double oven, one can be devoted to cooking the turkey and the second to cooking other items. This timetable is based on the following menu:

Buttered Roast Turkey (5.5 kg/12 lb stuffed weight) with Chestnut Stuffing
(made in advance, page 60)

Turkey Gravy
(stock made in advance, page 69)

Bacon and Chipolata Rolls
(prepared in advance and ready to bake, page 65)

Bread Sauce
(made on Christmas Eve, page 46)

Cranberry Kumquat Sauce
(prepared in advance, page 46)

Roast Potatoes
(page 72)

Baked Mustard and Orange Carrots
(page 74)

Creamed Brussels Sprouts with Chestnuts
(page 74)

Parsnip Dauphinoise
(prepared in advance and ready to bake, page 75)

8.00 am	Take the turkey out of the fridge and prepare as in the recipe. Leave at room temperature.
9.00 am	Prepare the vegetables so that they are ready for cooking.
9.30 am	Arrange the oven shelves so that the turkey will fit.
	Preheat the oven to Gas Mark 4/electric oven 180°C/fan oven 160°C.
10.00 am	Put the turkey in the oven and baste every hour.
10.15 am	Enjoy a champagne breakfast with your family!
11.00 am	Enlist some help to lay the table – it will be helpful if you lay one place setting as you would like the table to be laid.
11.30 am	Put any wine and drinks that need to be chilled in the fridge.
Midday	Start steaming the Christmas pudding, remembering to top up with water every 40 minutes.
12.15 pm	If you are having a cold starter, this is a good time to prepare it.
12.45 pm	Start the roast potatoes. Preheat the second oven or increase the temperature of your oven for the last half an hour or so of cooking the turkey.
1.05 pm	Put the roast potatoes in the oven.
1.20 pm	Remove the turkey from the oven and leave it to rest for 30 minutes, still covered in foil. Put the bacon and chipolata rolls, carrots and parsnips in the oven.
1.25 pm	Start cooking the sprouts and make the gravy.
1.45 pm	Finish the sprouts, reheat the Bread Sauce as well as the Cranberry and Kumquat Sauce.
1.50 pm	Carve the turkey and turn off the oven(s). Put the plates in the oven to warm.
1.55 pm	Put all the vegetables in serving dishes, cover and keep warm in the oven.
2.00 pm	Sit down with your guests and enjoy.

Vegetarian Christmas

I became a vegetarian about 18 years ago. Christmas was the first big hurdle as I always loved the traditional Christmas turkey with all the trimmings. Somehow I managed to survive my first vegetarian Christmas without giving in to turkey. Since then it has become easier. In those early days, nut roasts were the only option. Nowadays, vegetarian food has become far more imaginative and interesting.

In this chapter, I have included a number of vegetarian dishes suitable for the festive period. If you still hanker after a traditional roast with all the trimmings, then I would recommend the Chestnut and Mushroom Roast served with Glamorgan Sausages, Chestnut and Cranberry Stuffing Balls and Roasted Red Pepper and Tomato Sauce. If you love Italian food, as I do, then either the Italian Gateau or Holly's Christmas Filo Pie fit the bill.

Whatever you choose to make, I'm sure the meat-eaters at the table will ask if they can try a piece of yours!

Broccoli and stilton Roulade *(page 95)*

CHESTNUT & MUSHROOM ROAST

Nut roasts have become less popular over the years – as vegetarian food has become more interesting, they have seemed dull and dry by comparison. I was therefore keen to dispel that image and create a moist roast, full of flavour. As nut roasts are a little dull in appearance, a colourful sauce is needed to accompany it: I would recommend the Roasted Red Pepper Sauce (page 87). I am thrilled with the result – I hope you will be too.

Serves 6 Preparation time: 25 minutes Cooking time: 40–45 minutes

2 tablespoons olive oil

1 large onion, chopped finely

2 large carrots, chopped

1 teaspoon dried herbes de Provence

250 g (9 oz) field mushrooms, sliced

2 tablespoons finely chopped fresh parsley

5 tablespoons sherry

5 tablespoons light vegetable stock

200 g packet of whole cooked chestnuts

25 g (1 oz) chopped walnuts

1 egg, lightly beaten

50 g (2 oz) fresh breadcrumbs, plus extra if needed

butter for greasing

salt and freshly ground black pepper

1 Preheat the oven to Gas Mark 5/electric oven 190°C/fan oven 170°C.

2 Grease a 900 g (2 lb) loaf tin and line the base and narrow sides with baking parchment.

3 Heat the oil in a large saucepan and then fry the onion and carrots with the herbes de provence over a moderate heat with the lid on the saucepan for 10 minutes, stirring from time to time.

4 Add the mushrooms, parsley, sherry, stock, salt and pepper and continue to cook for a few more minutes.

5 Transfer the mixture to a processor or blender, with the chestnuts and walnuts, and blend to a fairly smooth purée.

6 Add the egg and breadcrumbs and mix together. If the mixture seems a little wet, add more breadcrumbs.

7 Transfer the mixture to the prepared tin and bake in the oven for 40 minutes or until it has set.

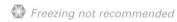 *Freezing not recommended*

Tip: To ensure that the slices don't disintegrate when you cut the roast, it is best to cook it, chill it, cut it into slices and then re-heat it.

SCC

PLACE NAMES

If you are having a dinner party, think about where to seat your guests. This is especially important if you have personalised gifts on the table. A good way to ensure that people sit where you want them to is to make place names.

If your dining table has a natural feel to it, then why not use decorated brown luggage tags, tying them to the base of each guest's glass with some Christmas ribbon? For a more sophisticated look, you could either make your own paper using one of the ideas in the book (see page 37), or visit your art shop for some gold or silver card. If you are really pushed for time, you could use a Christmas gift tag.

AG

ROASTED RED PEPPER AND TOMATO SAUCE

This is such a versatile sauce – it will liven up a dish and also makes a delicious pasta sauce. If you want a really smooth sauce, you'll need to sieve it. **Makes about 1 pint** Preparation time: 30 minutes

2 red peppers, quartered and de-seeded
1 shallot, chopped finely
1 garlic clove, chopped finely
1 tablespoon olive oil
400 g can of chopped tomatoes
150 ml (¼ pint) light vegetable stock
1 teaspoon balsamic vinegar
salt and freshly ground black pepper

1 Preheat the grill to a medium high heat. Place the peppers, skin side up, under the grill and grill until the skins are black. Place in a plastic bag and seal, or in a bowl and cover with cling film.

2 Fry the shallot and garlic in the oil until softened and beginning to brown.

3 Remove the skins from the peppers and cut the flesh into strips. Add the pepper strips to the shallot and garlic and fry for a few minutes, stirring occasionally.

4 Add the tomatoes, stock and seasoning. Bring to the boil and then simmer for a few minutes, stirring from time to time.

5 Remove from the heat and add the vinegar.

6 Transfer to a blender or food processor and blend until smooth.

7 Return to the saucepan and heat through. You may want to add some more vegetable stock if you require a thinner sauce.

Freezing: Cool, pour into a rigid container and cover with a lid. Thaw in the fridge overnight – thawing gradually will ensure the best results.

SCC

GLAMORGAN SAUSAGES

I think that sausages are the one things that vegetarians miss most when they give up eating meat. These little sausages, I hope you will agree, are a good substitute. They are called 'Glamorgan' because they are made in Glamorgan with Caerphilly cheese, and a very Welsh vegetable, leek. **Makes 10–12** Preparation time: 30 minutes

175 g (6 oz) fresh white breadcrumbs
115 g (4 oz) Caerphilly cheese, grated
1 small leek, shredded finely
2 tablespoons parsley, chopped finely
½ teaspoon mustard powder
1 large egg, beaten
1 egg white, lightly beaten
3 tablespoons plain flour
1 teaspoon mustard powder
sunflower oil, for frying
salt and freshly ground black pepper

1 Place the breadcrumbs, cheese, leek, parsley, mustard and seasoning in a large bowl and mix together. Add the egg and bind the mixture together. If it is a little dry, you may need to add a little milk.
2 Take a spoonful of the mixture and roll it into a sausage shape. Repeat with the remaining mixture.
3 Mix the flour with the mustard. Dip each sausage into the egg white and then into the flour.
4 Heat a little oil in a large frying pan and fry the sausages, a few at a time, over a moderate heat, turning them until they are crisp and brown all over.
5 Place the sausages on kitchen paper to remove any excess oil and then keep them warm while you cook the remaining sausages.

 Freezing not recommended

Tip: If, like me, you prefer your sausages really crisp on the outside, pop them into a hot oven for a few minutes after frying them.

SCC

CHESTNUT & CRANBERRY STUFFING BALLS

These are delicious and look pretty with the addition of the cranberries. Using cranberry sauce saves you poaching fresh cranberries and, I think, makes the stuffing nice and moist! **Makes about 15** Preparation time: 25 minutes Cooking time: 25 minutes

115 g (4 oz) fresh white breadcrumbs
1 small onion, chopped finely
1 tablespoon fresh parsley, chopped finely, or 1 teaspoon dried parsley
80 g (3 oz) cooked chestnuts, chopped
2 tablespoons cranberry sauce
1 egg, beaten
25 g (1 oz) butter, melted, plus extra for greasing
salt and freshly ground black pepper

 Freezing recommended

1 Preheat oven to Gas Mark 5/ electric oven 190°C/fan oven 170°C.

2 Place the breadcrumbs, onion, parsley, seasoning and chestnuts in a mixing bowl and stir to blend together the ingredients.

3 Add the cranberry sauce, egg and butter and mix thoroughly.

4 Grease a baking sheet. Shape the mixture into about 15 balls and place on the baking sheet.

5 Bake in the oven for about 25 minutes or until they are crisp and golden brown.

Freezing: Open-freeze on a tray and place in a freezer bag. They are best cooked from frozen although they will take a little longer, about 35–40 minutes.

SCC

WILD MUSHROOM PÂTÉ

The aroma in the house when preparing this pâté is wonderful! Using dried mushrooms intensifies the mushroom flavour. The pâté can either be presented in little ramekin dishes or in an attractive terrine. If you are giving the pâté as a present, it needs to be stored in the fridge until you give it. **Serves 6–8**
Preparation time: 40 minutes + 30 minutes soaking + cooling + 1 hour chilling

25 g (1 oz) porcini or forest mushrooms
150 ml (¼ pint) boiling water
50 g (2 oz) butter
1 small onion, chopped finely
2 large garlic cloves, chopped finely
450 g (1 lb) chestnut mushrooms, wiped with kitchen paper and sliced
1 tablespoon fresh thyme or 1 teaspoon dried thyme
250 g tub of ricotta cheese
1 tablespoon medium sherry

1 Put the dried mushrooms in a bowl and pour over the boiling water. Leave to soak for 30 minutes.

2 In the meantime, melt the butter in a saucepan and fry the onion and garlic over a moderate heat for about 10 minutes until the onion has softened but not coloured, stirring from time to time.

3 Add the chestnut mushrooms and thyme and fry for a further 10 minutes. In a fine sieve, strain the dried mushrooms into a bowl to remove any gritty particles, but retain the soaking liquid. Add the dried mushrooms and their soaking liquid, and simmer until all the liquid has evaporated. Allow to cool.

4 Spoon the mushroom mixture into a food processor and process with the ricotta cheese and sherry until it is the required texture.

5 Spoon into the chosen dish(es). Cover with cling film and chill for 1 hour.

 *Freezing not recommended*

SCC

MUSHROOM STRUDEL

This has to be my all-time favourite Christmas dish. I have been making it for a number of years and always get asked for the recipe. The Port Sauce on page 99 is the perfect accompaniment. I recommend Cypressa filo pastry (available at Waitrose) if you can get it, as it's the best I have come across.

Makes 2 strudels; serves 6
Preparation time: 30 minutes
Cooking time: 35 minutes + 30 minutes cooling

175 g (6 oz) butter

1 small onion, chopped finely

1 garlic clove, crushed

125 g (4½ oz) button mushrooms, sliced

150 g (5 oz) chestnut mushrooms, sliced

225 g (8 oz) flat mushrooms, halved and sliced

1 tablespoon sherry

1 teaspoon fresh thyme leaves or ½ teaspoon dried thyme

25 g (1 oz) fresh white breadcrumbs

25 g (1 oz) pine nuts, toasted

8 small sheets of fresh or frozen filo pastry

3 tablespoons cranberry sauce

1 tablespoon sesame seeds

salt and freshly ground black pepper

a few sprigs of fresh thyme, to garnish

1 Melt half of the butter in a large saucepan and fry the onion and garlic gently until soft. Add all the mushrooms and toss well in the onion and garlic. Fry for a few minutes until the mushrooms are cooked. Remove from the heat and stir in the sherry, thyme, breadcrumbs, pine nuts and seasoning. Allow to cool.

2 Preheat the oven to Gas Mark 6/electric oven 200°/fan oven 180°C.

3 Melt the remaining butter. Lay a clean tea towel on the work surface and arrange one sheet of filo pastry on top with one of the longest sides closest to you. Brush with some of the melted butter. Repeat until you have four layers of pastry.

4 Spread half the cranberry sauce evenly over the pastry. Spoon half the mushroom mixture along the side furthest away from you but leaving a gap at either end to fold over the filling. Fold the ends over the mushroom filling and then, using the towel to help you, roll the strudel towards you until all the mixture is enclosed in the pastry.

5 Carefully lift the strudel onto a large baking sheet. Brush with butter and sprinkle with half the sesame seeds.

6 Repeat to make the second strudel. Add the remaining sesame seeds to it.

7 Bake the strudel in the oven for 30–35 minutes until crisp and golden brown. If it seems to brown too quickly, cover loosely with foil.

 Freezing not recommended

Tip: You can prepare the dish a day in advance and simply cover it with cling film or foil and store it in the fridge.

SCC

ITALIAN GATEAU

Although the ingredients are not Christmas ones, the colours are festive. The gâteau also looks impressive, which I think is important for such a special meal. I made it to take to my friend Wendy's for dinner. As a vegetarian, she thought it would make a great dish for Christmas Day. It can be made a day in advance and cooked just before eating or cooked when made and simply reheated before serving. **Serves 4–6** Preparation time: 45 minutes Cooking time: 25–30 minutes

1 medium aubergine, sliced fairly thinly
1 large courgette, sliced fairly thinly, lengthways
6 tablespoons olive oil
1 onion, chopped finely
1 garlic clove, peeled and crushed
400 g can of chopped tomatoes
1 teaspoon sugar
1 teaspoon pesto sauce
3 red peppers, quartered and de-seeded
2 tablespoons plain flour
3 tablespoons freshly grated Parmesan cheese, plus extra to sprinkle on top
3 eggs, lightly beaten
a handful of fresh basil leaves
250 g pack of mozzarella cheese, cut into thin slices
salt and freshly ground black pepper

1 Place the aubergine and courgette slices in a colander, sprinkle with salt and place a weight on top. Leave for 30 minutes.

2 In the meantime heat 2 tablespoons of the olive oil in a saucepan. Fry the onion and garlic in it until soft. Add the tomatoes, sugar, salt and pepper and bring to the boil. Simmer for about 15 minutes until the sauce has thickened and there is no liquid left. Stir in the pesto, then set aside.

3 Preheat the grill to a medium high heat. Rinse the aubergines and courgettes and pat dry with kitchen paper.

4 Place the peppers under the preheated grill, skin side up, and grill until the skins have blackened. Place in a plastic bag and seal, or place in a bowl and cover with cling film.

5 Dip the aubergine and courgette slices in the flour.

6 Add the 3 tablespoons of Parmesan cheese to the eggs.

7 Dip the aubergine and courgette slices into the egg mixture and fry in the remaining olive oil until golden on both sides and cooked through. Drain on kitchen paper.

8 Remove the skin from the peppers and cut into strips.

9 Preheat oven to Gas Mark 5/ electric oven 190°C/Fan 170°C.

10 Lightly oil a 20 cm (8 inch) springform tin and assemble the gateau as follows. Arrange a third of the aubergine in the bottom in a single layer, add half of the courgettes followed by half of the pepper strips, a sprinkling of torn basil leaves, a third of the mozzarella and tomato sauce. Repeat the layers, finishing with the final layer of aubergine.

11 Sprinkle over the Parmesan cheese and bake the gâteau in the oven for 25–30 minutes until it is cooked through and the top is golden in colour.

 *Freezing not recommended*

Tip: It is important that the aubergine and courgette are sliced thinly and cooked thoroughly so that they are soft and malleable – once the gateau has been assembled, it's a good idea to press it down gently. Doing both these things will ensure that the gateau keeps its shape when the sides are removed and is easy to slice.

SCC

WINTER VEGETABLE AND CAERPHILLY CRUMBLE

The cream and wine add a touch of luxury to this satisfying vegetable crumble. The vegetables you use can be altered to suite tastes and availability. **Serves 6**
Preparation time: 30 minutes
Cooking time: 40 minutes

1 tablespoon olive oil

1 medium onion, peeled and diced

2 cloves garlic, peeled and crushed

3 medium leeks, trimmed and cut into thick slices

3 medium parsnips, peeled and cut into 2.5 cm (1 inch) cubes

1 small celeriac, peeled and cut into 2.5 cm (1 inch) cubes

275 g (9½ oz) chestnut mushrooms, halved if large

150 ml (¼ pint) good vegetable stock

300 ml (½ pint) dry white wine

1 heaped teaspoon corn flour, dissolved in a little water

150 ml (¼ pint) single cream

115 g (4 oz) cream cheese

80 g (3 oz) Caerphilly cheese, cubed

60 g (2½ oz) Parmesan cheese, freshly grated

60 g (2½ oz) fresh wholemeal breadcrumbs

1 Fry the onion and garlic in the oil until soft but not coloured. Add the leeks, parsnips and celeriac and cook gently for a few minutes. Add the mushrooms and cook for a few more minutes.

2 Add the stock and dry white wine, bring to the boil and then simmer gently for about 15 minutes until the vegetables have softened but still retain their shape.

3 Meanwhile, preheat the oven to Gas Mark 5/electric oven 190°C/fan oven 170°C. Stir in the dissolved corn flour to the vegetable mixture and continue stirring until thickened. Add the cream, cream cheese and Caerphilly cheese and stir until dissolved.

4 Spoon into a large ovenproof dish, sprinkle with Parmesan cheese and breadcrumbs that have been mixed together, then bake in the oven for 30–40 minutes until the sauce is bubbling and the top is golden brown.

SCC

BROCCOLI & STILTON ROULADE

This is such a pretty and impressive dish. It is also versatile since it can be served as a starter with some salad leaves, as a centrepiece for a buffet and also as a main course with a sauce such as Port (page 99) or rich tomato. **Serves 4**
Preparation time: 30 minutes
Cooking time: 15 minutes + cooling

For the roulade
225 g (8 oz) broccoli florets
40 g (1½ oz) butter
25 g (1 oz) plain flour
150 ml (¼ pint) milk
100 g (3½ oz) Stilton cheese, crumbled
3 large eggs, separated
salt and freshly ground black pepper

For the filling
250 g tub of cream cheese, at room temperature
50 g (2 oz) Stilton cheese, crumbled
2 tablespoons cranberry sauce, plus extra to serve

1 Preheat oven to Gas Mark 6/ electric oven 200°C/fan oven 180°C. Line a 20 x 30 cm (8 x 12 in) Swiss roll tin with baking parchment.
2 Cook the broccoli until it is tender. Drain and purée in a liquidizer or blender.
3 Place the butter, flour and milk in a saucepan and whisk over a moderate heat until sauce has formed. Simmer over a very gentle heat for a couple of minutes.
4 Remove from the heat and stir in the cheese until it has melted. Add the egg yolks, one at a time, and beat to incorporate them thoroughly. Fold in the broccoli purée and season with the salt and pepper.
5 Whisk the egg whites in a large bowl until they are stiff. Add a tablespoon to the broccoli mixture and beat in to loosen it. Fold in the remaining egg whites using a figure of eight action so that you don't knock out the air.
6 Gently spoon the mixture into the prepared tin, carefully level the surface and spread the mixture into the corners.
7 Bake in the oven for 15 minutes until the surface is golden and firm to the touch. Place a wire cooling rack on top and cover the rack with a damp tea towel. Allow to cool.
8 When cool, using the four corners of the parchment paper to help you, lift the roulade onto a large piece of greaseproof paper on the work surface. Peel off the baking parchment paper.
9 Spread the cream cheese over the surface, scatter the Stilton over this and then spread the cranberry sauce on top. With one of the long sides facing you, roll up the roulade using the paper to help you.
10 Cover the roulade with foil until ready to serve.
11 When ready to serve, place the roulade in a moderate oven in the foil to warm it through. Serve sprinkled with Parmesan cheese and extra cranberry sauce.

Freezing: Open freeze on a tray and then wrap in a freezer bag. Thaw overnight in the fridge.

SCC

STUFFED MUSHROOM & STILTON TART

I adore stuffed mushrooms and decided to create a tart using them. Arranging them in a circle in a tart case filled with a Stilton custard creates a stunning dish for a buffet table. For a dinner party starter, you could make eight individual ones with the stuffed mushroom in the centre of each tart. This is quite an involved recipe so I have suggested ready-made shortcrust pastry. **Serves 8** Preparation time: 40 minutes + 30 minutes chilling and cooling Cooking time: 30–35 minutes

350 g (12 oz) shortcrust pastry
9 x 8 cm (3 inches) open mushrooms, stalks removed
80 g (3 oz) fresh white breadcrumbs
2 tablespoons olive oil
1 tablespoon fresh thyme leaves or 1 teaspoon dried thyme
50 g (2 oz) fresh Parmesan cheese, grated
4½ cherry tomatoes, halved
300 ml (½ pint) single cream
3 eggs
1 egg yolk
80 g (3 oz) Stilton cheese, crumbled
salt and freshly ground black pepper
fresh thyme, to garnish

1 Preheat the oven to Gas Mark 5/ electric oven 190°C/Fan 170°C.
2 Roll out the pastry to a circle large enough to fit an 28 cm (11 inch) loose-bottomed flan tin. Roll the pastry around the rolling pin and unroll it into the tin. Press the pastry into the tin and trim the edges. Chill for 30 minutes.
3 Prick the base of the pastry with a fork. Line with greaseproof paper and baking beans and bake blind for 15 minutes. Remove the paper and beans and return to the oven for a further 5 minutes.
4 While the tart is in the oven, heat the oil in a large frying pan and fry the breadcrumbs and thyme for a few minutes until crisp and golden. Remove the pan from the heat and allow to cool.

5 Stir the Parmesan cheese into the pan and season. Divide the breadcrumb mixture between the mushroom cavities and top each one with half a tomato, cut side upwards.
6 Place eight of the mushrooms in a circle in the pastry case and the ninth in the centre.
7 Whisk the eggs, egg yolk and cream together until just blended. Season. Pour the custard very carefully into the pastry case, in between the mushrooms, and then scatter the Stilton cheese on top of the custard.
8 Bake the tart in the oven for 30–35 minutes until the custard has set and both the custard and mushrooms are golden in colour. garnish with fresh thyme.

 *Freezing not recommended*

Tip: If serving as a starter, try roasting some vine cherry tomatoes and serve them on the side as a delicious and refreshing accompaniment.

SCC

HOLLY'S CHRISTMAS FILO PIE

This recipe is dedicated to Holly as these are her favourite ingredients – we'll therefore be enjoying this on Christmas Day. I will serve it with a roasted tomato sauce for her and I'll prepare the Port Sauce (opposite) for myself (you should have the food you like on this special day!). You can vary the vegetables to suit the tastes of your guests. **Serves 6**
Preparation time: 40 minutes
Cooling time: 30 minutes
Cooking time: 40 minutes

1 butternut squash, weighing about 700 g (1½ lb)
350 g (12 oz) chestnut mushrooms, wiped and halved
1 red onion, chopped roughly
2 carrots, diced
1 courgette, sliced thickly
2 tablespoons olive oil
2 garlic cloves, peeled and crushed
a handful of fresh basil leaves
350 g pot of fresh tomato sauce, such as Neapolitan
80 g (3 oz) butter, melted
½ x 250 g pack of filo pastry
salt and freshly ground black pepper

1 Preheat oven to Gas Mark 7/ electric oven 220°C/fan oven 200°C.
2 Peel the butternut squash, cut in half, remove the seeds and fibrous middle, and then cut the flesh into small cubes.
3 Place the squash in a large (you may need two) roasting tin, add the other vegetables with the garlic. Sprinkle the oil all over the vegetables and season with the salt and pepper.
4 Roast in the oven for 30 minutes until the vegetables are just tender and beginning to brown. Tear the basil leaves and add them to the vegetables.
5 Pour over the tomato sauce and mix in thoroughly. Allow to cool.

6 Grease a 20 cm (8 inch) cheesecake (spring-release) tin with a little of the melted butter. Place a sheet of the pastry in the tin, allowing the edges to hang over. Brush the pastry sheet with some butter and continue to line the base of the tin with the filo sheets overlapping them like the spokes of a wheel. The edges should hang over the sides.
7 Spoon the filling into the tin and then carefully lift the overlapping pieces of pastry, one at a time and brush with butter, to enclose the filling. Brush the surface liberally with the remaining butter.
8 Bake in the oven for 40 minutes. You will probably need to cover the top with foil before the end to prevent it from getting too brown.

Freezing: Open freeze on the tin base and then place in a freezer bag. Cook from frozen but you will need to add an extra 10 minutes or so to the cooking time.

SCC

PORT SAUCE

This is a natural partner for the Mushroom Strudel (page 90). I often make double the quantity because it's so popular. The reduction is the key to the success of the sauce as it concentrates the flavours. **Serves 6–8** Preparation and cooking times: 25 minutes

25 g (1 oz) butter

1 small onion, chopped finely

2 tablespoons plain flour

700 ml (1¼ pints) good vegetable stock

a small sprig each of fresh thyme and parsley

2 bay leaves

1 tablespoon tomato purée

2 tablespoons ruby port

salt and freshly ground black pepper

1 Melt the butter in a saucepan and fry the onion for a few minutes until it has softened and is golden brown.

2 Stir in the flour and stir well to incorporate it. Continue to cook over a gentle heat until the mixture starts to brown.

3 Remove from the heat and gradually stir in the stock, stirring well between each addition.

4 Return to the heat and bring to the boil, stirring to prevent any lumps forming.

5 Add the herbs, tomato purée and seasoning. Boil for a few minutes until the sauce has reduced by about half to approximately 425 ml (¾ pint).

6 Strain the sauce into a clean saucepan, add the port and bring to the boil. Simmer for a couple of minutes, then check the seasoning.

Freezing: Pour the sauce into a plastic tub and cover it with a lid.

SCC

RIBBON CARDHOLDER

A simple idea for displaying your cards is to make a ribbon cardholder. This can be used year after year if you remove the old cards carefully, or you can change the ribbon depending on your Christmas theme or colour scheme.

You will need:

- wide ribbon as long as the piece of wall you want to hang it from. If you can't get wide ribbon, try joining two pieces together, either by sewing them or by making a feature of the join with beads or hand embroidery.
- a bow added to the top of the cardholder (see Gift Bows, page 78) or a small decoration with an inverted "V" cut at the bottom.

Staple your cards down the sides of the cardholder, either leaving gaps where the ribbon will show or covering the ribbon completely.

AG

SUN-DRIED TOMATO SAUCE

This is a versatile sauce and worth making double quantities so that you have some in your freezer for an instant meal with pasta or vegetables. **Serves 4–6** Preparation time: 30 minutes

2 tablespoons olive oil (preferably from the sun-dried tomato jar)

1 small onion, peeled and finely chopped

1 clove garlic, chopped

400 g tin tomatoes

4 sun-dried tomatoes, in oil, drained and sliced thinly

2 tablespoons balsamic vinegar

150 ml (¼ pint) light vegetable stock

1 Fry the onion and garlic in the oil over a moderate heat until soft.

2 Add the tomatoes, bring to the boil and reduce the heat so that the sauce simmers gently.

3 Season with salt and pepper and cook, uncovered, for about 15 minutes.

4 Add the sun-dried tomatoes and then pour the mixture into a blender or food processor.

5 Blend until smooth adding the stock in stages until the required consistency is reached.

6 Add the balsamic vinegar and check the seasoning.

 Freezing recommended

To Freeze: Cool and then pour into a rigid container. Cover with a lid.

SCC

CRANBERRY AND PORT SAUCE

Serves 4 Preparation time: 10 minutes.

450 g (1 lb) cranberries

90 ml (3½ fl oz) red wine

45 ml (3 tablespoons) fresh orange juice

80 g (3 oz) sugar

2 tablespoons arrowroot, dissolved in 30 ml water

60 ml (4 tablespoons) port

150 ml (¼ pint) single cream

1 Place the cranberries, orange juice, wine and sugar in a saucepan. Bring to the boil and simmer for 3–4 minutes until the cranberries are tender.

2 Stir in the arrowroot and jelly and cook until thickened. Add the port and cream. Taste and add more sugar, if needed.

 Freezing not recommended

SCC

FABRIC BASKET

This can be adapted in many ways, depending on what you plan to use it for and the materials or trimmings you choose to decorate the basket. It could be used on the table for bread rolls and cheese biscuits, Christmas crackers or as a basket for handmade gifts. The instructions below are for a basket with a base of 22 x 22 cm (8½ x 8½ inches), but you can alter this to any size you like. You will need:

- two squares of fabric, each 44 cm x 44 cm (17½ x 17½ inches). This could be a material that is suitable for using all year round or something special for Christmas.
- 8 ties, each about 25 cm (10 inches) long made from the same fabric, stitched into tubes and turned through, or from ribbon in a complementary colour, to give a nice full bow, a little shorter for something less fancy.
- firm base for your basket. This could be some thin card or pelmet Vilene, cut to the finished size, in this case 22 x 22 cm (8½ x 8½ inches).

1

1 To make the basket, pin a tie 4 cm (1½ inches) in from each corner of one of your fabric squares on the right side, and with the 'raw' edges together, stitch these in place.

2

2 Place the second square on top, with right sides together, and stitch round three sides using a 1 cm (½ inch) seam allowance. Take care not to get the ties caught in the seams. Turn the fabric through and insert your base. Turn the edges of the fourth side under and stitch together.

3

3 Carefully manoeuvre the base until it is in the centre of the square, then pin and top stitch it into place.

4 Iron and tie the edges together to complete the basket.

AG

Cheat's
Christmas

It's great to make your own food, but at this hectic time of year, we all need to strike a balance – we're all for a bit of clever cheating to make life easier. It's a case of making good use of quality convenience/ready-prepared ingredients and giving them a personal touch.

We've taken a few short-cuts in this chapter, cheated a bit to create some delicious festive dishes that guests will be convinced you made yourself from scratch, spending hours in the kitchen! There are recipes for each course as well as hot and cold options, and many can either be prepared in advance and/or frozen, saving even more time.

Caramelised Tropical Fruit Brochettes *(page 118)*

CHICKEN LIVER PÂTÉ WITH BRANDY & GARLIC MUSHROOMS

This quick and easy pâté can be served on its own with Melba toast or on crusty bread, but adding the garlic mushrooms and a few salad leaves creates another interesting flavour combination. **Serves 4 as a starter** Preparation and cooking time: 35 minutes + cooling

125 g (4½ oz) butter

1 small onion, chopped finely

1 garlic clove, crushed

225 g (8 oz) tub of chicken livers

1 tablespoon brandy

¼ teaspoon dried thyme or mixed herbs

salt and freshly ground black pepper

Garlic mushrooms

50 g (2 oz) butter

250 g (9 oz) button mushrooms, sliced finely

2 garlic cloves, crushed

4 slices of herb bread, toasted

salt and freshly ground black pepper

1 Make clarified butter: melt 25 g (1 oz) of the butter over a low heat and continue cooking until it is foaming well. Pour the butter into a basin and leave it to settle. Skim off any foam and leave until quite cold.

2 Melt 25 g (1 oz) of butter in a sauté pan, cook the onion and garlic until soft, and then add the chicken livers. Increase the heat and sauté briskly for 2–3 minutes, when the liver should be firm to the touch but still retaining a hint of pink colour inside.

3 Cool the mixture. Put it into an electric blender and blend until you have a smooth consistency.

4 Add the remaining butter and blend into the liver mixture. Season well and mix with the brandy and herbs.

5 Put the liver pâté into a china dish or small terrine dish. Smooth over the top. Melt the clarified butter and pour it over the top of the pâté.

6 Leave to set and keep refrigerated until ready to use.

7 To make the garlic mushrooms, melt the butter in a pan, add the mushrooms and garlic and cook quickly, stirring for about 5 minutes. Season with salt and pepper.

8 Put a spoonful of the mixture onto a slice of herb bread and serve.

❄ *Freezing: Place the finished pâté in a freezer bag, seal and freeze. Thaw in a refrigerator.*

Tip: This pâté mixture can also be used to make a terrine. Use slices of prosciutto ham to line a loaf tin and fill with the pâté. Turn out when set.

MEW

WILD MUSHROOM & ARTICHOKE PIE

Isn't it wonderful to be able to create a meal in minutes that looks and tastes as if you've slaved for hours over a hot stove? This dish fits the bill. It's simply a case of opening some quality ingredients, combining them and cooking some ready-made pastry in the oven.

Serves 4 Preparation time: 10 minutes Cooking time: 15–20 minutes

375 g packet of ready-rolled puff pastry

1 egg, beaten

a handful of sesame seeds

400 g can of Forest Mushroom Mix (I used 'Borde'), drained

350 g tub of Wild Mushroom Sauce

390 g can of artichoke hearts, drained and cut in half

300 g can of flageolet beans, drained

115 g (4 oz) baby sweetcorn, cut in half lengthways

1 Preheat oven to Gas Mark 6/ electric oven 200°C/fan oven 180°C.

2 Unroll the pastry and cut it into eight squares. Mark the surface of the squares with a diamond pattern using the tip of a sharp knife. Place the squares on a baking sheet, brush with the egg and scatter sesame seeds on top. Bake in the oven for 15–20 minutes until puffed and golden.

3 Just before the pastry is ready, empty the Mushroom Mix, Wild Mushroom Sauce, artichoke hearts, flageolet beans and sweetcorn into a saucepan and bring to the boil, stirring. Simmer over a gentle heat for a few minutes until the sweetcorn is just tender.

4 To serve, place a pastry square on each plate, spoon the filling over and place another pastry square on top.

Freezing: Spoon the filling into a plastic tub with a lid and freeze. Freeze the pastry separately and thaw them both in the fridge overnight. Continue from step 3, but you'll have to heat the pastry in a warm oven.

SCC

PRAWNS WITH AVOCADO & FENNEL

Pale green fennel has the delicate flavours and aroma of aniseed and gives an excellent crunchy texture to this simple-to-put-together starter. **Serves 8**
Preparation time: 20 minutes

150 g (5 oz) pack of ready-prepared Bistro salad leaves e.g. lamb's lettuce, shredded beetroot, red chard

1 bulb of Florence fennel, trimmed and cut into fine strips (see Tip)

2 ready to eat avocados, stoned, peeled and cut into slices

250 g (9 oz) cooked, peeled tiger prawns

125 ml (4½ fl oz) ready-made Italian salad dressing

2 tablespoons chopped fresh dill

freshly ground black pepper

To serve

8 lemon twists

8 cooked fresh prawns in shells

8 slices of brown bread

softened butter, to spread on bread

1 Arrange the salad leaves on eight plates.

2 Divide the fennel, avocados and prawns over the salad leaves and season with freshly ground black pepper.

3 Drizzle 2 tablespoons of the dressing onto each salad and scatter dill over the top.

4 Garnish with a twist of lemon and a prawn on each salad. Butter the bread slices and then cut into triangles to serve.

 Freezing not recommended

Tip: If you have never used fennel, buy a firm unblemished bulb with a tuft of feathery green fronds at the top. To prepare the fennel, remove the outer layer if it is damaged, cut away the stalks at the top and trim a thin slice from the base. Cut the fennel into quarters and slice finely into strips.

MEW

COUSCOUS SALAD WITH HARISSA DRESSING

This impressive starter will appeal to those who like their food a little spicy. There are so many good ingredients, such as roasted peppers, available in jars these days – it makes it easy to create quality dishes such as this one in minutes, saving you time in the kitchen. If you can't find peppers stuffed with feta cheese, simply use plain ones and incorporate about 50 g (2 oz) of diced feta cheese.

Serves 4 Preparation time: 25 minutes

100 g sachet of couscous (I used Ainsley Harriot's 'Spice Sensation Couscous')
4 roasted red peppers, stuffed with feta cheese (from a jar)
6 black olives, stoned
1 teaspoon harissa paste
100 g (3½ oz) Greek yoghurt
a handful of rocket salad leaves

1 Prepare the couscous according to the packet instructions.
2 While the couscous is absorbing the water, cut the peppers and olives into small pieces. Lightly oil four ramekin dishes and line the bases with discs of baking parchment.
3 Stir the harissa into the yoghurt.
4 When the couscous is ready, add the diced, stuffed peppers and olives and stir to combine evenly.
5 Spoon the couscous mixture into the prepared ramekin dishes and gently press down. Invert the ramekins into the centre of four serving plates, lift off and remove the paper discs. Present as moulds or fluff the couscous with a fork if you prefer.
6 Place a spoonful of dressing in the centre of the couscous and surround it with rocket leaves.

 Freezing not recommended

Tip: If you don't feel confident about turning the couscous out of the ramekin dishes, you could either use small rings or simply spoon it on to each plate.

SCC

RÖSTI-TOPPED HALIBUT WITH SMOKED SALMON & AVOCADO

Halibut has an excellent flavour and thick firm flesh making it an ideal choice for a main course fish dish. The joy of this recipe is that it takes no time to put together yet looks so good. Cheat by using a packet of Rösti mix for the potato cakes. **Serves 4** Preparation time: 30 minutes Cooking time: 30 minutes

butter for greasing

4 x 175 g (6 oz) skinned halibut fillets

8 tablespoons natural yogurt or crème fraîche

100 g (3½ oz) smoked salmon, sliced thinly

1 ready-to-eat avocado pear, quartered

juice of 1 lemon

50 g (2 oz) Parmesan cheese, grated finely

salt and freshly ground black pepper

To serve

1 packet of frozen ready-made rösti

a little olive oil

225 g (8 oz) crisp green beans or broccoli

1 Preheat oven to Gas Mark 4/ electric oven 180°C/fan oven 160°C.

2 Butter a shallow ovenproof dish. Put the halibut in the dish in a single layer and season with salt and pepper.

3 Spread 2 tablespoons of yogurt or crème fraîche over each fillet and top with smoked salmon.

4 Make a fan of the avocado by cutting each quarter into slices up to two thirds of the way down and then spread it out like a fan on top of the smoked salmon. Sprinkle with lemon juice and then Parmesan cheese.

5 Bake for approximately 30 minutes.

6 Cook the rösti according to the packet instructions and place it on top, or to the side, of each fillet before serving. Drizzle with a little olive oil to serve.

7 Serve with some crisp green beans or broccoli.

 *Freezing not recommended*

MEW

BEEF IN BEER WITH PRUNES

This is the perfect recipe to have ready in advance if you are entertaining, as it tastes better when it is made the day before, allowing the rich dark sauce to blend with the meat. Much of the work is done for you if you cheat by buying the ingredients ready prepared from the supermarket. Serves 6

Preparation time: 15 minutes
Cooking time: 3 hours

1 x 500 ml (18 fl oz) bottle of beer (such as Theakston's Black Sheep Ale)
1 beef stock cube, crumbled
1 teaspoon mixed dried herbs
1 tablespoon wholegrain mustard
2 tablespoons cornflour
1 tablespoon garlic paste
¼ teaspoon allspice
¼ teaspoon nutmeg
1 tablespoon unrefined molasses sugar
2 x 454 g packs of lean, diced casserole beef
225 g (8 oz) drained pickled onions
1 x 480 g pack of ready-prepared casserole vegetables (to include carrots, leeks and turnips)
20 ready to eat prunes
4 squares of dark chocolate
1 tablespoon chopped parsley
salt and freshly ground black pepper

1 Preheat oven to Gas Mark ½/ electric oven 120°C/fan oven 100°C.
2 Put the beer, beef stock cube and herbs into a flameproof casserole, bring to the boil and simmer for 5 minutes.
3 In a small basin, blend together the mustard, cornflour, garlic paste, allspice, nutmeg, and sugar with a little water. Add this mixture to the casserole and bring to the boil, whisking until thickened.

4 Add the beef, onions and vegetables. Season with salt and pepper.
5 Cover and cook for approximately 3 hours or until the meat is tender.
6 Add the prunes and chocolate 20 minutes before the end of the cooking time.
7 Serve sprinkled with chopped parsley.

 Freezing recommended

Tips: Top the casserole with caraway seeds or herb dumplings to ring the changes.

To re-heat next day, put in the oven at Gas Mark 2/electric oven 150°C/fan oven 130°C for 40–45 minutes. To freeze, cool, pack in a polythene box and seal. To thaw, place in the fridge overnight and reheat as above for serving.

MEW

APPLE, MINCEMEAT & ALMOND CRUMBLE

Few people can resist a crumble at this time of year. This one combines seasonal ingredients that go so well together. Serve with a good quality ready-made custard, to which you've added a splash of brandy – heaven!

Serves 4–6 Preparation time: 10 minutes Cooking time: 20–25 minutes

350 g (12 oz) can of apple slices
400 g (13 oz) mincemeat
225 g packet of luxury crumble mix
115 g (4 oz) marzipan
50 g (2 oz) flaked almonds

1 Preheat oven to Gas Mark 5/ electric oven 190°C/fan oven 170°C. Lightly grease an ovenproof dish.
2 Empty the apple slices and mincemeat into the dish and mix with a spoon to combine.
3 Empty the crumble mix into a bowl and grate or crumble the marzipan into it. Stir to combine and then spoon over the mincemeat mixture.
4 Level the surface and then scatter the flaked almonds on top.
5 Bake for 20–25 minutes until the crumble is cooked and golden.

Freezing: Freeze before cooking and then cover with foil and place in a freezer bag. Thaw at room temperature and then cook as above.

SCC

MISTLETOE BALL

Decking the house with mistletoe and kissing underneath it is an ancient custom – it may even date back to the Druids, who considered it a magical plant with sacred properties. Branches would have been hung outside doors as a sign of forgiveness. This may be where the phrase "kiss and make up" comes from.

Take care if you have small children helping, because even though birds and other wildlife love mistletoe berries they are poisonous to humans.

1 Buy a bunch of mistletoe and cut it into short stems.
2 Make holes in the potato with a skewer and insert the stems into them, so that the potato is covered completely. The moisture from the potato will keep the mistletoe fresh. The potato can be sliced or shaped as required.

AG

BANOFFEE TARTS

Banoffee Pie is so very popular but rather time-consuming to make. I have therefore created this cheat's version, which takes minutes to make AND tastes delicious. Who needs to know that you didn't make it from scratch? **Serves 4** Preparation time: 20 minutes + optional warming of sauce

4 rich-butter shortcake dessert bases
1 large banana
4 tablespoons banoffee sauce
150 ml (¼ pint) double cream
sifted cocoa powder, to dust
1 dessert spoon chocolate truffle sauce (optional)

1 Place the shortcake bases on serving plates.

2 Peel and slice the banana and divide between the cases, arranging the slices neatly.

3 Spoon or squeeze the banoffee sauce over the banana slices.

4 Whip the cream until it holds its shape. You can either spoon the cream over the filling or put it into a piping bag and pipe it onto create a professional finish.

5 Dust the cream with the cocoa powder.

6 If you're using the chocolate sauce, warm it so that it is a fairly runny consistency. Serve the chocolate sauce separately or see Tip for a more professional finish.

Tip: Put dots on the plates at equal intervals around the tarts. Using a toothpick or skewer, place the tip in the centre and pull outwards to create a teardrop effect.

 Freezing not recommended

PARTY WREATH

This wreath can be hung on a wall or door, or used as a table centrepiece. Either re-use an old wreath or make your own as described here.

You will need:
- a small gift for each guest
- labels or wrapping paper; one design for ladies, another for gentlemen
- old wire coat hanger
- ivy or pine branches
- tape or floral wire
- Christmas decorations or ribbons or holly berries or fir cones or lights or a combination

1 To make the wreath, begin by bending an old wire coat hanger into a ring shape. You could either cut off the hook, or cover it, together with the rest of the wreath, and use it for hanging.
2 Cover the ring with ivy or small pieces of pine branch attached with tape or floral wire, working around the ring in overlapping layers. You might want to add ribbons or christmas decorations, holly berries, fir cones, or even tiny battery powered lights, depending on where your wreath is to go. If you have a theme to your party, the wreath could be decorated with items that tie in with the theme.

3 For each guest you will need a gift or surprise. These should be reasonably small and light as they will be tied on to the wreath. Gifts can be something personal, in which case they should be labelled, or something appropriate for either a male or female guest. In the latter case you should wrap the gifts in such a way that nobody goes home with an inappropriate surprise. Wrap male and female gifts differently, then let your guests pick a gift from the wreath or you can hand the gifts out as your guests leave.

AG

CARAMELISED TROPICAL FRUIT BROCHETTES

A hot dessert is a treat, but this one is simple to make and a complete contrast to the usual rich puddings that are produced at Christmas. It's also an interesting way to enjoy fresh fruit or you could use a selection of prepared fruit with others of your choice. **Serves 4**
Preparation and cooking time: 30 minutes + 20 minutes soaking + 15 minutes for chocolate physalis (optional) + setting

8 wooden bamboo skewers
4 fresh figs
2 firm and just ripe bananas
2 just ripe Asian pears
1 small pineapple
1 pawpaw
2 kiwi fruit
1 star fruit
juice of 1 lemon
8 teaspoons unrefined demerara
   sugar
1 jar of passion fruit and mango
   coulis
scoops of ice cream (coconut
   flavour is excellent)
To decorate (optional)
physalis (cape gooseberries),
   dipped in melted bitter dark
   chocolate

1 Soak the wooden bamboo skewers in cold water for 20 minutes.
2 Preheat the grill to a medium high heat.
3 Prepare the fruit as necessary and cut it into attractive bite-sized pieces. Thread it onto skewers, alternating the fruits to make a colourful brochette.
4 Sprinkle the brochettes with half the lemon juice and half the sugar and grill for 2–3 minutes until lightly caramelised. Turn over, sprinkle with the remaining lemon juice and sugar, and continue to grill for a further 2–3 minutes.

5 For each serving, put two fruit brochettes onto a flat plate and drizzle round the coulis. Serve hot, with scoops of ice cream.
6 For real luxury, decorate with physalis, dipped in bitter dark chocolate. To make chocolate physalis: carefully peel back the sepals and then hold each berry by its 'wings' and dip it into the melted chocolate. Leave the physalis to set on baking parchment.

 Freezing not recommended

Tip: These chocolate physalis are also good served with coffee after dinner.

MEW

RASPBERRY & YOGURT CRUNCH

This recipe is loosely based on the Scottish dish, Crowdie. It takes very little time to put together and looks good served in stem glasses to show off the individual layers. **Serves 8**
Preparation time: 10 minutes + 10 minutes chilling

1 x 500 g (1 lb 2 oz) tub of Greek-
   style natural yogurt with honey
grated rind of 1 lemon
2 tablespoons clear honey
1 tablespoon Drambuie
175 g (6 oz) toasted crunchy cereal
   (such as Jordan's Luxury Crunchy
   Golden Honey and Nut)
450 g pack of fresh raspberries
   (save 8 to use as decoration)
8 mint leaves

1 Mix together the yogurt, lemon rind, honey and Drambuie. Stir in the cereal.
2 Layer the raspberries and yogurt mixture in eight tall glasses. Decorate each with the remaining raspberries and the mint leaves.
3 Chill for about 10 minutes before serving.

 Freezing not recommended

Tip: You can use frozen raspberries but don't let them defrost completely before using them in order to retain their shape. If you like your fruit a little sweeter, dust the raspberries with icing sugar before layering.

MEW

Christmas Brunches

Breakfast is such a personal and individual meal – you are either one of those who cannot start the day without it, or one of those who cannot face food first thing.

Brunches are a different matter – they are popular with most people, particularly when you get the chance to start the day in a leisurely way. Over Christmas, brunches are a great idea, especially if you don't want to spend time preparing meals three times a day. By combining breakfast and lunch you can save yourself a lot of work and be popular with your family, who may want to lie-in!

In this chapter there are familiar dishes, such as kedgeree, as well as some more unusual ideas, such as the Baked Brioche filled with Creamy Wild Mushrooms (page 124). Whatever you choose to make, when served with traditional breakfast ingredients such as cereals, bread and fruit, these meals will sustain your family and guests until dinner.

Double Decker Christmas Special Sandwich *(page 126)*

SCRAMBLED EGGS WITH ROQUEFORT

Adding Roquefort cheese to scrambled eggs changes this from an everyday snack to something special. Spreading the toast with sun-dried tomato paste complements the cheese and eggs beautifully. **Serves 4** Preparation and cooking time: 10 minutes

8 eggs, preferably free-range

4 tablespoons single cream

25 g (1 oz) butter, plus extra for the toast

salt and fresly ground black pepper

100 g (3½ oz) Roquefort cheese

4 thick slices of bread, preferably from an uncut loaf

4 teaspoons sun-dried tomato paste

cherry tomatoes, to garnish

1 Crack the eggs into a bowl and whisk lightly with a fork. Add the cream and stir in. Season sparingly with the salt and pepper, keeping in mind that Roquefort is a salty cheese.

2 Melt the butter in a saucepan and swirl to cover the base completely.

3 Add the egg mixture and cook over a gentle heat, stirring often.

4 While the eggs are cooking, make the toast. Butter the toast and spread it with the sun-dried tomato paste. Place the toast on plates and put into a warm oven.

5 When the eggs have just cooked, remove from the heat and crumble in the cheese. Spoon the cheesy scrambled eggs onto the toast and garnish with cherry tomatoes.

 *Freezing not recommended*

SCC

WRAPPING IVY

Old Man's Beard or ivy is often available from park and hedgerows at Christmas time.

You will need:
- craft paint
- paper tablecloth or napkins
- fine fuse wine

1 If the leaves of the ivy are damp, let them dry out.

2 When dry, spray them with craft paint by either laying them on a plain paper tablecloth or on napkins in the same way as we described for wrapping paper (page 37). Then your cloth will be decorated too!

3 When the foliage is ready to use, it can be wrapped around bottles, pinned round church candles, laid on the table or used in wreaths. If the stems are too stiff, you may need to wire them so that they stay in place. You will find them much easier to control if you wrap fine fuse wire around the stems. Remember to trim inflammable material so that it doesn't catch in the flame.

AG

KEDGEREE

Kedgeree is an old-fashioned breakfast dish consisting of smoked haddock and cooked rice. It originated in India and was brought back to the UK by British Colonials at the end of the Raj. It has enjoyed something of a revival in recent years because it is such a versatile dish and is a good choice for brunch. **Serves 8**
Preparation and cooking time: 45 minutes

350 g (12 oz) basmati rice
½ teaspoon turmeric
700 g (1 lb 9 oz) smoked haddock
milk, to cover
2–3 lemon slices
2 teaspoons cumin seed
2 teaspoons crushed coriander
5 cm (2 inch) cinnamon stick
50 g (2 oz) butter
250 g (9 oz) onions, chopped
1 garlic clove, crushed
400 g (14 oz) can green lentils or
    yellow split peas
2 hard-boiled eggs
150 ml (¼ pint) fresh single cream
    (optional)
25 g (1 oz) fresh coriander
salt and freshly ground black
    pepper
To serve
lemon wedges
mango chutney

1 Boil a pan of slightly salted water. Add the rice and turmeric and cook for 8–10 minutes until tender and all the liquid has been absorbed.

2 Poach the haddock in the milk with the lemon slices until just cooked. Use a fish slice to lift the fish from the liquid and set it aside to cool. Keep the poaching liquid. Remove all the skin and bones from the haddock and flake the flesh.

3 In a dry frying pan, over a low heat, shake the cumin, coriander and cinnamon until they begin to release their fragrance. Put to one side.

4 Melt the butter in a pan and fry the onion and garlic until the onions are soft and pale. Remove from the heat and stir in the rice, spices and lentils or peas. Gently fork in the flaked fish and the hard-boiled eggs. Season with salt and pepper to taste.

5 Return to the heat for 2–3 minutes. If the kedgeree is not moist enough, add some of the poaching liquid from the fish or alternatively the single cream.

6 Fork through the fresh coriander and put the kedgeree into a warm serving dish. Serve with lemon wedges and mango chutney.

 Freezing not recommended

Tip: To make another attractive garnish, fry an onion with 2 teaspoons of garam masala and scatter this over the top of the kedgeree just before serving.

MEW

BAKED BRIOCHES FILLED WITH CREAMY WILD MUSHROOMS

Brioche rolls are so attractive that they make perfect cases for the mushrooms. This is a very stylish brunch dish (which can also be served as a starter) – it looks so professional that you will be sure to impress your guests! **Serves 4** Preparation and cooking times: 20 minutes + 12 minutes

4 brioche rolls

50 g (2 oz) butter

1 shallot, chopped finely

1 garlic clove, chopped finely

250 g (9 oz) wild mushrooms (e.g. oyster, shiitake, morels)

1 tablespoon brandy

1 tablespoon fresh tarragon, chopped or 1 teaspoon dried tarragon, plus extra to garnish

200 ml (7 fl oz) crème fraîche

salt and freshly ground black pepper

1 Preheat oven to Gas Mark 6/ electric oven 200°C/fan oven 180°C.

2 Place a brioche on its flat base, carefully cut off the top and, using a sharp knife, cut out the centre of each roll, leaving a shell of about 1 cm (½ inch). Repeat with the other rolls.

3 Melt 15 g (½ oz) of the butter and brush it on the insides of the cases and the lid. Place the rolls and their lids on a baking sheet and bake in the oven for 10–12 minutes until they are crisp and golden.

4 While the rolls are in the oven, melt the remaining butter and fry the shallot and garlic until the shallot has softened.

5 Add the mushrooms and cook gently for 5 minutes. Add the brandy, tarragon, seasoning and crème fraîche. Cook for a few minutes, stirring frequently, until the sauce has reduced and thickened.

6 Fill the brioche rolls with the warm mushroom mixture and garnish with extra tarragon. Serve with salad leaves, if you like.

 Freezing not recommended

SCC

DOUBLE DECKER CHRISTMAS SPECIAL SANDWICH

The secret of a good double-decker sandwich is to provide an appetizing contrast in tastes and textures. Don't forget the napkins, as it is impossible to eat these without getting messy.

Serves 4 Preparation time: 20 minutes

For the French toast

2 eggs, beaten

2 tablespoons milk

butter, for frying

12 slices of bread, cut from a
    square, medium-sliced
    sandwich loaf

For the fillings

shredded lettuce leaves, such as
    Cos

2 tomatoes, sliced

1 red onion, sliced thinly into rings

8 teaspoons mayonnaise

8 thin slices of turkey breast

12 slices of Brie

8 teaspoons cranberry sauce

To serve

relishes, chutneys or pickles

1 To make the French toast mix the egg and milk together and season. Melt the butter and heat until hot and foaming. Dip each slice of bread in the egg mixture and fry it in the butter.

2 To make the layered sandwich, place some shredded lettuce on one piece of French toast. Top this with 2 teaspoons of mayonnaise and a few slices of tomato and onion, then season with salt and pepper.

3 Place a second piece of toast on top. Place 2 slices of turkey breast with 2 teaspoons of cranberry sauce, then 3 slices of Brie on top. Cover this with a third piece of toast.

4 Cut diagonally in half with a sharp knife and secure each half with a cocktail stick.

5 Serve accompanied by relishes, chutneys or pickles.

 *Freezing not recommended*

Tip: If you want to make things very easy and informal, put the various fillings in separate dishes, give your guests a stack of French toast and let them choose.

MEW

GLASS BALL ORNAMENTS

This is a good way to use your old or scratched glass baubles, so you don't have to buy new ones! Most of these ideas can also be used with clear plastic baubles.

You will need:

- glass or clear plastic baubles (plastic baubles are a better option for younger children)

To fill baubles

- tinsel, beads, sequins, glitter or tiny sweets or Christmas spices

To decorate baubles

- glue and gutta or black glitter and glass points (from an art or craft shop)

1 To recycle old baubles, soak them in bleach for a few minutes and rinse them in warm soapy water. This will remove most of the silvering from inside the ball, but you may need to use a cotton bud to complete the job. Don't forget to wear rubber gloves when using bleach.

2 Once you have a clear bauble, you can remove the top and fill it with anything appropriate to your Christmas theme or colour scheme. Remember not to fill it with anything too heavy or the branches of your tree may not support it.

It may help to make a funnel by rolling a piece of paper so that one end is narrow enough to fit inside the ball. Place tape along the edge to hold the funnel together. Now fill the bauble with scraps of tinsel, coloured beads, sequins, glitter or tiny sweets.

3 Create layers of colour and texture by filling baubles with spices such as ground nutmeg, crushed cinnamon sticks, or cloves. Alternatively, you could fill them with lavender or crushed potpourri.

4 If using plastic baubles, paint glue on the outside of the ball and roll it in glitter.

If using glass baubles you can draw designs on with black glass gutta and fill in the shapes with glass paints to give a stained glass effect. Bands of colours work well, or you could paint on tiny spots or other geometric shapes. (this idea cannot be applied to plastic baubles because the plastic might melt)

AG

PORK SAUSAGES WITH CARAMELISED ONION GRAVY

Bangers and mash is a very English dish but relies for its appeal on using the very best sausages. Traditionalists will go for the good old fashioned chunky porker, full of meat and seasoning, but you can now buy local specialities at the many Farmers' Markets around the country. **Serves 4** Preparation and cooking time: 25 minutes

For the sausages

8 good quality pork sausages

oil, for brushing

For the caramelised onion gravy

25 g (1 oz) unsalted butter

1 tablespoon sunflower oil

500 g (1 lb 2 oz) onions, peeled and sliced thinly

1 teaspoon caster sugar

2 tablespoons red wine vinegar

1 tablespoon plain flour

250 ml (8 fl oz) stock

salt and freshly ground black pepper

1 tablespoon chopped parsley, to garnish

1 Brush the sausages lightly with oil, but don't prick them. (This will keep them succulent.) Fry or grill the sausages for about 8–10 minutes on each side until they are golden brown all over and starting to turn sticky on the outside. Do not try to cook them too quickly or the skins may split.

2 To make the onion gravy, melt the butter and oil in a sauté or frying pan. Add the onions and cook over a fairly high heat, stirring frequently until they start to brown.

3 Add the caster sugar and red wine vinegar, cover the pan and continue to cook gently for approximately 10 minutes until soft and caramel in colour, stirring occasionally.

4 Remove from the heat and sprinkle in the flour, then slowly add the stock and bring to the boil. Simmer for a few minutes until the gravy is thick and shiny. Season with salt and pepper and keep warm until ready to serve.

5 Sprinkle with chopped parsley to serve.

 Freezing not recommended

MEW

WARM MUSHROOM & SPINACH SALAD

This salad is not only full of flavour, it is also packed full of goodness, which is a welcome change during the Christmas period when everyone tends to over-indulge on unhealthy foods. The addition of the chilli gives the mushrooms a bit of a kick but it can be left out if you don't like spicy food. **Serves 4**
Preparation time: 25 minutes

15 g (½ oz) butter

1 red pepper, cut into strips and de-seeded

250 g (9 oz) chestnut mushrooms, wiped and sliced

115 g (4 oz) oyster mushrooms, torn in half

a pinch of cumin seeds

1 red chilli, de-seeded and chopped finely

1 ripe avocado pear, sliced

225 g (8 oz) baby spinach leaves, washed

salt and freshly ground black pepper

Parmesan shavings, to serve

For the vinaigrette

3 teaspoons extra virgin olive oil

1 teaspoon white wine vinegar

a pinch of sugar

salt and freshly ground black pepper

1 Melt the butter in a large frying pan and fry the pepper over a gentle heat for a few minutes until it has softened.

2 Add the mushrooms, cumin seeds and chilli and continue to cook for a few more minutes until they have softened. Season with the salt and pepper.

3 Place the vinaigrette ingredients in a large bowl and whisk together.

4 Toss the spinach in the vinaigrette and arrange on four serving plates.

5 Scatter the avocado on top and spoon the mushroom mixture, together with the juices, onto the spinach.

6 Scatter some Parmesan shavings on top and serve straightaway.

 Freezing not recommended

Tip: Wash your hands thoroughly (or wear latex gloves) after cutting the chilli and be sure not to touch your face as the membrane and seeds can burn your skin. Take care not to add the chilli membrane or seeds to the mushrooms as they are the hottest parts.

SCC

GIFT TAGS

All of the card ideas can be applied to making matching gift tags, but here are two other ways of decorating papers to use in any of the projects.

You will need:
- tea bag
- photocopier paper
- incense stick (optional)
- a bowl of water

or
- coloured tissue paper
- photocopier paper
- PVA glue
- goldfinger paste (available from most craft shops)

'Aged' paper

1 To make 'aged' papers, take a tea bag and soak it in boiling water, you can now use it like a sponge to dab over some ordinary photocopier paper for a mottled brown effect.

2 If you have access to a computer, type out the words to your favourite Christmas Carol over and over until you have filled a page, then print this on to the tea-coloured paper. Use an old-style font such as Blackadder ITC, Edwardian Script ITC or Harrington, in whatever size you prefer.

3 To give an extra aged feel to the paper, burn the edges with an incense stick. Make sure you have a bowl of water to hand when doing this in case of accidents!

Textured paper

Take some coloured tissue paper and scrunch it up well, then smooth it out taking care not to smooth out the crumples too much as you will loose the textured look. This can then be glued onto some more photocopyer paper – PVA glue works best. When the paper is completely dry, lightly rub some Goldfinger paste over it.

AG

MUSTARD MASH

This is delicious with the Pork Sausages with Caramelised Onion Gravy (page 128).

Serves 4 Preparation time: 25 minutes Cooking time: 20–25 minutes

1 kg (2 lb 4 oz) floury potatoes (e.g. King Edwards, Maris Piper) peeled and cut into large equal pieces
200 ml (7 fl oz) milk
50 g (2 oz) butter
25 g (1 oz) grated mature Cheddar cheese
2–3 tablespoons wholegrain mustard
salt and freshly ground black pepper

1 Cook the potatoes in lightly salted boiling water. Cover and simmer for 20–25 minutes until tender.

2 Drain and return the potatoes to the pan. Mash well with a potato masher.

3 Heat the milk and butter gently in the microwave oven until the butter melts (or use a small saucepan). Pour the butter into the mash and beat thoroughly using a wooden spoon until the mash is light and fluffy.

4 Beat in the grated cheese, add the mustard and stir through.

 Freezing not recommended

MEW

MUFFIN TOASTIES

Muffins make an excellent base for toasties and the ideas below can all be made in minutes.
Serves 8 Preparation and cooking time: 10–15 minutes

4 muffins, split and toasted
For the egg and salmon
2 eggs, hard-boiled and chopped roughly
2 tablespoons mayonnaise
1 teaspoon chopped chives
50 g (2 oz) smoked salmon trimmings
salt and freshly ground black pepper

1 Mix the eggs with the mayonnaise and chives. Season with salt and pepper.
2 Put the egg mixture on top of each muffin half, followed by smoked salmon.

For the bacon and Brie
8 rashers of streaky bacon, grilled and halfed
2 ripe pears, each cut into 8 slices
8 slicess of Brie

1 Put two slices of bacon on top of each muffin half, then add two slices of of pear and top with two slices of Brie.
2 Grill until the Brie begins to melt.

For the steak and Stilton special
1 teaspoon Dijon mustard
50 g (2 oz) butter
4 minute steaks, halfed
100 g (3½ oz) Stilton cheese
To serve
1 teaspoon chopped parsley
a few salad leaves
4 slices of tomato

1 Work the Dijon mustard into the butter and spread it on the toasted muffin halves.
2 Grill the steaks and place on the muffins.
3 Top with Stilton and then grill until the Stilton begins to melt.
4 Garnish with chopped parsley and serve with salad leaves and slices of tomato.

 Freezing not recommended

MEW

LEEK & SWEET POTATO TORTILLA

The tortilla is a Spanish open omelette as opposed to the frittata which is Italian. Tortillas usually include potato and so for a bit of a variation, I created this one using sweet potato. In addition to being tasty, the orange potato discs look so attractive. You could replace the leek with another green vegetable such as broccoli or asparagus. I like to serve the tortilla straight from the pan at the table. **Serves 4–6**
Preparation and cooking time: 30 minutes

450 g (1 lb) sweet potato, peeled and sliced 1 cm (½ inch) thick
2 tablespoons olive oil
2 leeks, trimmed and sliced thinly
5 eggs
4 tablespoons double cream
8 sun-blush tomatoes, snipped or cut into small pieces
115 g (4 oz) Gruyère cheese, grated
salt and freshly ground black pepper

SCC

1 Cook the potato slices in boiling water for about 5 minutes until they are just cooked, then drain them.

2 Meanwhile, heat the oil in a large frying pan and fry the leeks over a moderate heat, stirring occasionally until they have softened but not coloured.

3 Remove from the heat and arrange the potato slices in a single layer on top.

4 Whisk the eggs and cream together and season with the salt and pepper.

5 Add the tomato pieces and pour over the leeks and potatoes. Return to a lowish heat and cook until the tortilla is set on the bottom.

6 In the meantime, preheat the grill. Sprinkle the cheese evenly over the tortilla and grill until the cheese has melted and the tortilla is golden.

Freezing not recommended

PINECONES

Pinecones can be used for many decorations and ornaments at Christmas. They can be added to wreaths, hung from the Christmas tree, used on the table, or tiny ones can be used to decorate presents.

You will need:
- pinecones
- glitter, gold, silver or white spray or fabric pen
- card or ribbon, to hang (optional)
- glue gun or screw and thread (optional)

1 Clean the cones before use to remove any dirt and insects that may have collected in them. They can then be conditioned in the oven.

2 To do this, place them on a baking tray covered with tin foil and bake them in the oven at Gas Mark 6/electric oven 200°C/fan oven 180°C for a few minutes; the time will vary according to the size of the cones. This will melt the sap, giving the cones a nice glaze. Any cones that have not opened will open in the heat.

3 The cones are now ready to be decorated. They could be sprayed in glitter, gold, silver or white, or you could just paint the tips with a fabric pen.

4 If the cones are to be hung, you will need to attach a piece of cord or ribbon once they are decorated. You can either glue the ribbon in place with a glue gun or for larger cones, poke a small hole in the top and insert a screw with an 'eye'. Twist the screw into the pinecone to secure it well and thread the ribbon through the eye of the screw.

AG

Christmas
Leftovers

We're sure we're not alone in hating to waste food and we will do anything to avoid throwing away leftovers. In fact, some of our culinary successes have resulted from using up leftover food. As it's so difficult to know how much your family and guests will eat, and you want to make sure there is enough food on offer, it is inevitable that you will end up with food left over.

When you look in the fridge after Boxing Day, and wonder what on earth to do with all that leftover food, we hope the recipes in this chapter will inspire you. In fact, we hope you'll like them so much that you'll deliberately prepare too much to be sure you have the necessary leftover ingredients!

Mincemeat and Marzipan Ice Cream *(page 152)*

POTTED BLUE CHEESE WITH WALNUTS

The traditional recipe for potted cheese is usually Cheshire cheese and butter, but I like to use a blue cheese such as Wensleydale and add some cream cheese, often flavoured with chives. I serve this with rough oatcakes and slices of a crisp eating apple. **Serves 6–8** Preparation time: 15 minutes + chilling + standing

225 g (8 oz) Blue Wensleydale
    cheese, crumbled
125 g (4$\frac{1}{2}$ oz) cream cheese
125 g (4$\frac{1}{2}$ oz) unsalted butter,
    softened
3 tablespoons white Port
$\frac{1}{4}$ teaspoon ground mace
1 tablespoon chopped chives
50 g (2 oz) walnut halves
salt and freshly ground black
    pepper

1 Beat the cheese and butter to a paste.
2 Add the Port, mace and chives and beat again until smooth.
3 Season to taste.
4 Spoon the cheese into a serving dish.
5 Arrange the walnut halves on top.
6 Cover and refrigerate until firm.
7 Before serving, remove from the fridge and leave to stand until the potted cheese comes back to room temperature.

 Freezing not recommended

MEW

TRIPLE VEGETABLE TERRINE

Reheating leftover vegetables is rarely appetising. However, using the leftover vegetables from Christmas lunch is both delicious and attractive in this terrine – a good reason to make too much in the first place! **Serves 6** Preparation and cooking time: 20 minutes + 1$\frac{1}{4}$ hours + cooling

butter, for greasing
a handful of dry, finely grated
    Parmesan cheese to coat the
    loaf tin
350 g (12 oz) creamed sprouts with
    chestnuts
350 g (12 oz) julienne carrots,
    puréed
350 g (12 oz) celeriac purée with
    onions and mustard seeds
1 tablespoon crème fraîche
2 tablespoons fresh coriander,
    chopped finely
3 large eggs, beaten separately
salt and freshly ground black
    pepper

1 Preheat oven to Gas Mark 4/ electric oven 180°C/fan oven 160°C.

2 Grease the long sides of a 1 kg (2 lb) loaf tin with butter and line the base and narrow sides with a strip of baking parchment paper. Dust all the surfaces with the Parmesan.

3 Place the three vegetable purées in separate bowls. Add the crème fraîche and coriander to the carrots and add a beaten egg to each bowl. Season the carrot mixture with salt and pepper (the other two have already been seasoned).

4 Spoon the sprout mixture into the base of the prepared tin and level the surface. Follow with the carrot mixture and then finally with the celeriac.

5 Pour boiling water into a roasting tin to create a *bain marie* (water bath) and place the tin in the centre.

6 Bake in the oven for about 1¼ hours, until it is firm to the touch and a skewer comes out clean when inserted into the middle of the terrine. Allow to cool before turning out.

Freezing not recommended

SCC

CHRISTMAS SOAP

You can get ordinary glycerine soap in a variety of colours from chemists or craft shops. Here is an idea for personalising it with added 'bits', either for your own use over Christmas or to give as a present.

You will need:
- glycerine soap in colour(s) of your choice
- small dried leaves, flowers or pieces of citrus fruit. These should be dried before you start.
- small plastic or rubber ice cube moulds in Christmas shapes

1 Cut the desired amount of glycerine soap and place it in heavy-duty plastic bags. These bags should be placed in boiling water and simmered for 3–5 minutes until the glycerine has melted.

2 Place your dried leaves, flowers or fruit in the bottom of the ice cube moulds. Cut away a corner of the plastic bag and pour the melted glycerine over the top. You could create a layered look by half filling the moulds and leaving them to set before adding more fruit and soap. You could also try a layered effect using different coloured soaps.

3 Make sure your Christmas soap has cooled completely and hard before turning it out of the moulds.

AG

BRIE, ASPARAGUS & ROCKET PASTA SALAD

If you can't find asparagus fiorelli, which are like round ravioli, simply use a cheese-filled ravioli. All you need to accompany this dish is some crusty Italian bread, such as ciabatta, and a glass of chilled white wine. The salad can be eaten with a fork so it's the sort of informal supper you could have on a tray in front of the television as you relax after a busy Christmas. **Serves 4**
Preparation and cooking time: 15 minutes

250 g packet of asparagus fiorelli or
    cheese-filled ravioli
200 g packet of asparagus tips
4 teaspoons red pepper tapenade
2 tablespoons extra virgin olive oil
225 g (8 oz) Brie, cubed
16 baby plum tomatoes, halved
a packet of rocket salad leaves
Parmesan cheese, grated (optional)

1 Cook both the fiorelli and asparagus according to the packet instructions and drain well. Place in a bowl.
2 Mix the tapenade and oil together and pour over the pasta and asparagus. Add the Brie and tomatoes and season with salt and pepper.
3 Arrange the rocket leaves on four serving plates and spoon the pasta mixture on top, making sure that each plate has a fair share of each of the ingredients. Sprinkle with Parmesan cheese, if you like.

 Freezing not recommended

SCC

RED PEPPER CHEESE SOUFFLÉS

Soufflés always look spectacular so don't be afraid to make one. Think of it as adding eggs to white sauce and what could be simpler? This recipe is a good way of using up bits of left-over cheese and stuffing and it looks so colourful. Serve either as a starter, with foccacia, or as a light supper dish with salad.

Serves 4 Preparation time: 45 minutes Cooking time: 30 minutes

15 g (¹⁄₂ oz) melted butter

4 large and square red peppers

1 leek, shredded finely, or use cooked leftovers

350 g (12 oz) jar of cheese sauce (such as Lloyd Grossman Four Cheese sauce)

¹⁄₂ teaspoon dry mustard

¹⁄₄ teaspoon cayenne pepper

¹⁄₂ teaspoon dried oregano

3 eggs, separated

75 g (2³⁄₄ oz) Gruyère or Cheddar cheese, grated

4 balls (about 100 g/3¹⁄₂ oz) leftover cooked stuffing, crumbled (use the Chestnut Stuffing, page 48)

2 tablespoons freshly grated Parmigiano Reggiano

salt and freshly ground black pepper

1 Preheat the oven to Gas Mark 6/ electric oven 200°C/fan oven 180°C.

2 Lightly grease a shallow ovenproof dish with the melted butter.

3 Slice the tops of, each pepper reserving them if you wish, discard the core and seeds and place both the peppers and their tops in an ovenproof dish.

4 Cook the leek in lightly salted boiling water until soft, then drain.

5 Empty the cheese sauce into a large bowl and season with mustard, cayenne pepper, oregano, and plenty of salt and pepper as the addition of the egg white later will dull the flavour.

6 Stir in the egg yolks, grated cheese and cooked stuffing.

7 Whisk the egg whites until they form peaks (you should be able to hold the bowl upside down and not lose its contents!). Stir 1 tablespoon of egg white into the cheese sauce then gently fold in the rest with a large metal spoon.

8 Spoon half the mixture into the pepper cases; add the cooked leeks, then top with the remaining mixture. Sprinkle with Parmigiano Reggiano.

9 Run a sharp pointed knife inside the rim of each pepper and place them in the oven to cook for 30 minutes, until the soufflé is well risen, golden on top and just wobbly.

10 Serve immediately, with the baked pepper tops to the side, if desired.

 Freezing not recommended

MEW

BUBBLE & SQUEAK GRATIN

Bubble and squeak is an old favourite, usually made with left over cabbage and potatoes. In this dish, the cabbage is replaced with Brussels sprouts and then topped with sliced tomatoes and grated cheese to make it a tasty supper meal using Christmas leftovers.

Serves 4 Preparation and cooking time: 40 minutes

675 g (1½ lb) potatoes, cooked and mashed

350 g (12 oz) Brussels sprouts, cooked and mashed

25 g (1 oz) butter

1 onion, chopped finely

3 tomatoes, sliced

80 g (3 oz) mature Cheddar cheese, grated

salt and freshly ground black pepper

1 Combine the potatoes and sprouts and season with the salt and pepper.

2 Melt the butter in a large frying pan and fry the onion for about 5 minutes until it has softened and is beginning to turn brown.

3 Add the potato and sprout mixture, flatten with the back of a spatula and fry over a moderate heat for about 10 minutes, stirring frequently until browned.

4 While it is cooking, preheat the grill to a medium high heat.

5 Arrange the tomato slices on top and scatter the grated cheese evenly on top. Grill until the cheese has melted and is golden brown. Serve straight away.

 Freezing not recommended

SCC

CHESTNUT, STILTON & SPINACH STUFFED PANCAKES

When I set about creating this recipe, using left-over stuffing, I didn't expect something so delicious. Now I make stuffing just so that I have an excuse to prepare this dish. You could make your own pancakes if you wish, but I think that when Christmas is over, we all want to spend as little time as possible in the kitchen. **Serves 4** Preparation time: 35 minutes + Cooking time: 15–20 minutes

butter, for greasing

1 tablespoon olive oil

1 onion, chopped finely

350 g (12 oz) fresh spinach, or half this amount if using frozen spinach

4 pancakes

4 heaped teaspoons cranberry sauce

115 g (4 oz) stuffing (chestnut and herb is ideal)

50 g (2 oz) Stilton cheese, crumbled

½ quantity of Roasted Pepper and Tomato Sauce (page 87)

50 g (2 oz) grated Gruyère or Cheddar cheese

1 Preheat oven to Gas Mark 4/ electric oven 180°C/fan oven 160°C.

2 Lightly grease a rectangular ovenproof dish – I used one that is 16 x 23 cm (6¼ x 9 inches).

3 Heat the oil in a pan and fry the onion for a few minutes until it is soft. Add the spinach and continue to cook until the spinach has wilted (if using fresh spinach) or it has softened (if using thawed, frozen spinach).

4 To assemble, place the pancakes on the work surface. Spread a teaspoon of cranberry sauce on each pancake and divide the spinach mixture between them, arranging it down the centre.

5 Divide the stuffing and Stilton into four equal portions and scatter on top of the spinach mixture.

6 Bring one pancake side over the filling and then the other and place in the dish, seam side down. Repeat with the other pancakes.

7 Spoon the sauce over the pancakes and sprinkle with cheese.

8 Bake in the oven for 15–20 minutes until cooked through and the cheese topping is golden brown.

 Freezing not recommended

SCC

SOAP POWDER SNOWMAN

This is a project that small children will love and one in which they can get really messy!

1 First prepare a base for your snowman. This could be a piece of coloured card, some tin foil wrapped over a board, a cake plate or an old CD.

You will need:

For the base:

- coloured card, tin foil-wrapped board, cake plate, or old CD

For the snowman:

- 225 g (8 oz) soap powder plus extra for sprinkling
- cloves
- peppercorns
- orange card

2 To make the snowman, mix about 225 g (8 oz) of soap powder with 40 ml (1½ fl oz) of water (this may vary depending on the soap powder, but you will need to have a fairly stiff mixture). You can then make two balls of "snow", one slightly larger than the other.

3 Put the snowman's body on the base you have prepared and rest the head on top. You should be able to get the two to stick together fairly easily.

4 To make the snowman's eyes and buttons, use cloves, a row of small peppercorns for a mouth and a small triangle of coloured orange card for the "carrot" nose. You can make a hat by resting a bottle top on a circle of coloured card and make a scarf from some old fabric.

5 To complete the snow scene once it is in place, sieve some more soap powder round the base and over the snowman.

AG

DECORATED JARS AND BOTTLES

Pretty glass jars can be found in most kitchen shops and you could decorate any size or shape to use with biscuits or homemade sweets. The jar or bottle is a gift in itself and can be used long after the contents have been eaten. For fruit in syrup or alcohol, it is best to use a kilner jar with a secure lid and for flavoured oils, use a bottle with a secure lid.

See recipes for Apricots in Brandy, page 146 and Olive Oil with Chilli and Garlic, page 147. The glass paints and gutta are available from most art or craft shops in a good variety of colours.

You will need:
- a kilner jar
- some ribbon
- a glass bottle
- glass paints
- gutta

The gutta comes in a small tube, which you can use like a tiny icing bag to squeeze the paste onto the glass in fine lines.

- note paper
- a small envelope
- some Christmas ribbon

1 Decide what you're going to draw on the jar or bottle – something simple works best, perhaps some stars or Christmas trees, and draw the outline on the jar with the gutta. When the gutta is dry it will act as a barrier for the paint, so make sure you don't leave any gaps. The motifs can then be filled in with the glass paints.

2 When the paint is dry, you can fill the jar with delicious Apricots in Brandy (page 147) and the bottle with Olive Oil with Chilli and Garlic (page 146).

3 Finally copy the recipe onto notepaper, put it in a small envelope. For a really professional finish, you could copy a tiny version of your motif onto the front of the envelope or even decorate your notepaper in the same way. Punch a hole in the corner of the envelope and tie it around the jar or bottle with some Christmas ribbon.

AG

APRICOTS IN BRANDY

Fruits in liquor are a good store-cupboard standby for an instant dessert and also make a delightful gift for family and friends. *Serves 4–6* Preparation time: 15 minutes + overnight soaking + 3 weeks storage

a sterilised jar (see Tip)
225 g (8 oz) whole dried apricots
juice of 1 large orange or 4
    tablespoons fresh orange
    juice
100 g (3½ oz) granulated sugar
100 ml (3½ fl oz) brandy
ice cream or Greek yogurt, to
    serve

You will need a half-litre kilner jar (available from most hardware stores)

1 Soak the apricots in 700 ml (18 fl oz) water with the orange juice overnight.
2 Drain the liquid from the apricots and measure 300 ml (½ pint) into a saucepan. Arrange the apricots in a sterilised jar.
3 Make a light syrup by dissolving the sugar in the drained liquid. Bring to the boil for 2 minutes, then cool.
4 Add the brandy to the syrup and pour over the fruit, making sure that all the fruit is covered.
5 Seal, cool and store in a cool place for 3 weeks before using.

 Freezing not recommended

Tip: To sterilise the jar, wash in hot soapy water, then rinse thoroughly in very hot water and drain. Put the jar onto a baking sheet and place in an oven preheated to Gas Mark 3/ electric oven 140°C/fan oven 120°F for 10 minutes, then remove and cover with a clean tea towel until ready to use.

MEW

OLIVE OIL WITH CHILLI AND GARLIC

Flavoured oils make lovely gifts and are so simple to make. To prepare as a gift, tie a label around the neck of the bottle with raffia. To add a little something extra, attach a set of measuring spoons.

The flavoured oil can be used as a dressing or as a marinade for vegetables, fish or meat will keep for up to 3 months. **Makes 250 ml (9 fl oz)** Preparation time: 5 minutes + 1–2 weeks infusing.

wide-necked jar with plastic screw top, sterilised (see Tip on page 144)
250 ml (9 fl oz) good quality mild olive oil
a few bay leaves
3 garlic cloves, peeled and halved
12 peppercorns, crushed roughly
6–8 chilli peppers
To finish:
tomato ketchup/or re-use a oil bottle, sterilised (see Tip on page 144)
6–8 whole dried chilli peppers
6–8 whole red peppercorns
3 bay leaves
1 garlic clove, peeled and chopped

1 Ensure that the seal on the jar is airtight.
2 Pour the oil into a wide-necked jar and add the bay leaves, garlic, peppercorns and chilli peppers. Make sure that they are below the surface of the oil.
3 Cover and leave for 1–2 weeks to infuse, shaking the jar each day.
4 Strain into the bottle and throw away the flavourings.
5 Add the chilli peppers, bay leaves, garlic clove and peppercorns for decoration. Seal and store in a cool place.

 Freezing not recommended

MEW

TURKEY STIR-FRY

A stir-fry is a good way to use up left-over turkey and is one of the quickest and easiest of dishes to make. **Serves 4** Preparation and cooking time: 35 minutes

1 red pepper, cored and seeds removed, then sliced

1 orange pepper, cored and seeds removed, then sliced

5 cm (2 inch) piece of fresh root ginger, peeled and cut into matchsticks

125 g (4$\frac{1}{2}$ oz) baby sweetcorn, halved

125 g (4$\frac{1}{2}$ oz) mangetout, ends trimmed and halved diagonally

2–3 spring onions, root and top removed

1 can of bamboo shoots in brine, drained

100 g (3$\frac{1}{2}$ oz) dried medium egg noodles

3 tablespoons light soy sauce, plus extra for serving

2 tablespoons rice wine (or use a medium-dry sherry)

1 tablespoon clear honey

3 tablespoons stir-fry oil

200 g (7 oz) diced left-over cooked turkey pieces

50 g (2 oz) cashew nuts

8 chive stalks, to garnish

1 Put the peppers, ginger, sweetcorn, mangetout, spring onions and bamboo shoots in separate bowls.

2 Put the noodles in a bowl and pour in boiling water to cover. Leave to soak for a few minutes until tender. Drain the noodles into a colander and rinse with cold running water to prevent them from sticking together.

3 Whisk together the soy sauce, rice wine and honey in a bowl.

4 Put the wok on the hob and spoon in 2 tablespoons of the oil. Heat for about 1 minute until there is a faint smoky blue haze.

5 Put in the peppers, the remaining 1 tablespoon of oil, the ginger and then the sweetcorn. Mix well and continue stir-frying for about 4 minutes.

6 Stir in the soy sauce mixture, then the mangetout and bamboo shoots and continue to stir-fry.

7 Shake the noodles and add them to the wok with the turkey and nuts. Stir-fry until heated through and mixed in.

8 Serve at once in warm bowls with extra soy sauce. Lay two chive stalks on top of each bowl to serve.

 Freezing not recommended

Tip: For a successful stir fry, prepare all the ingredients before you start cooking.

MEW

ORIENTAL HAM CASSEROLE

This is a delightful, tasty supper dish, light but satisfying, with a unique blend of flavours. It is complemented by the crisp vegetables and is best served on a bed of long grain rice. **Serves 4** Preparation time: 25 minutes + Cooking time: 45 minutes

350 g (12 oz) cooked ham, cut into chunks

1 medium-sized onion, thinly sliced into rings

1 large green pepper, de-seeded and sliced into rings

150 g (5½ oz) tin of pineapple pieces in natural juice

100 g (3½ oz) raisins

300 ml (½ pint) pineapple juice

4 tablespoons vinegar

100 g (3½ oz) light muscovado sugar

1 tablespoon cornflour

¼ teaspoon salt

freshly ground black pepper

1 tablespoon soy sauce

boiled rice, to serve

1 Put the ham in a casserole dish.

2 Arrange the onion, green pepper, pineapple and raisins on top of the ham.

3 Heat the pineapple juice with the vinegar.

4 Blend the sugar, cornflour and salt and pepper together.

5 Pour a little of the hot juice onto the blended paste and stir in.

6 Return the paste to the liquid in the saucepan and heat gently, stirring until it thickens.

7 Add the soy sauce and pour the liquid into the casserole. Cook at Gas Mark 6/electric oven 200°C/ fan oven 180°C for about 45 minutes.

8 Serve the casserole with boiled rice.

 Freezing not recommended

MEW

GOLDEN MERINGUE QUEEN OF CHRISTMAS PUDDINGS

If you don't know what to do with the left-over Christmas pudding, try this adaptation of a traditional favourite. **Serves 4**
Preparation time: 30 minutes + 20–30 minutes soaking + Cooking time: 1 hour

4–6 slices of Christmas pudding
15 g ($\frac{1}{2}$ oz) butter
300 ml ($\frac{1}{2}$ pint) milk
15 g ($\frac{1}{2}$ oz) sugar
grated rind of $\frac{1}{2}$ lemon
2 egg yolks
2 tablespoons ginger marmalade
1 whole piece of stem ginger, chopped
2 tablespoons syrup from the ginger jar
For the meringue
2 egg whites
125 g ($4\frac{1}{2}$ oz) golden caster sugar

1 Grease the top rim of a 600 ml (1 pint) ovenproof dish. Preheat the oven to Gas Mark 4/electric oven 180°C/fan oven 160°C.
2 Break up the left-over Christmas pudding.
3 Boil the butter with the milk, drop the Christmas pudding into it, add sugar and lemon rind and put a lid on the saucepan. Leave to soak for 20–30 minutes.
4 Beat the egg yolks into the Christmas pudding and milk and turn the mixture into the pudding dish.
5 Bake for 20–30 minutes until it is just set.
6 When set, take the dish from the oven, spread the ginger marmalade over it and add the stem ginger and 2 tablespoons of syrup from the ginger jar on top. Reduce the oven to Gas Mark 1/ electric oven 140°C/fan oven 120°C.
7 Whisk the egg whites until stiff, then whisk in 2 teaspoons of sugar and finally fold in the rest of the sugar with a tablespoon. Pile the meringue on top of the pudding.

8 Put the pudding back into the cool oven for 20–25 minutes to dry the meringue and make it crisp.
9 Serve hot.

 Freezing not recommended

Tip: Meringue can be cooked by the 'flash method'. Bake at Gas Mark 6/electric oven 200°C/fan oven 180°C for 10 minutes until golden brown.

MEW

MINCEMEAT & MARZIPAN ICE CREAM

I created this ice cream one Christmas when I had some mincemeat and marzipan left over. It takes minutes to prepare but tastes as if a lot of time has been spent making it! It is delicious served with Fruit Compote (page 54). **Serves 4–6** Preparation time: 15 minutes + cooling + at least 2 hours freezing + 15 minutes softening

115 g (4 oz) marzipan, cut in pieces
600 ml (1 pint) double cream
6 tablespoons mincemeat
2 tablespoons Amaretto liqueur
    (you could substitute brandy or
    whisky)

1 Place the marzipan and cream in a saucepan and cook over a gentle heat until the marzipan has melted.

2 Stir well and then add the mincemeat and Amaretto and mix well. Allow to cool.

3 Place in a plastic tub, cover and freeze with the freezer set on 'fast freeze'.

4 After an hour or so, when the ice cream has begun to freeze, remove it from the freezer and stir well so that the fruit is distributed evenly. Freeze for another hour or until solid.

5 Remove the ice cream from the freezer 15 minutes before serving to allow it to soften slightly.

 Freezing recommended

SCC

GIFT BAG

This is a simple way of making an individual bag for a gift using chosen paper or some you have made yourself (page 37). You make this just as if you were wrapping a box but turn one end under and leave loose – then take the box out and add handles.

You will need:
- a box the right size for your gift (so it is a good idea to keep a collection of boxes of various sizes)
- paper
- card, to fit bottom of gift bag
- hole punch
- pretty ribbon or card for handle
- tissue paper

1

1 Cut the paper to the height you want the finished bag, then add another 7 cm (3 inches) at the top and enough at the bottom to wrap the cover of the box. Turn the top of the paper 7 cm (3 inches) to the inside crease and stick it. This will give a neat edge to the top of the bag. Wrap the paper around the box, as if wrapping a present. Fold over about 1 cm (½ inch) along the outside edge and stick it, using double-sided tape.

2

2 Fold the bottom ends of the bag over the box as if you were wrapping a present and tape this in place. Now you can slide the bag off the box.

3

3 Cut a piece of card to fit inside the bottom to make the box sturdier and punch holes in the top for a pretty ribbon or cord handle. For a nice finishing touch, fill the bag with tissue paper and add your gift.

AG

Parties and Celebrations

Gone are the days when hosting a party meant working so hard that you didn't enjoy yourself or were unable to spend as much time with your guests as you would like. With careful planning and plenty of advance preparation, this should no longer be the case – throwing a party should be as much fun as going to one!

The emphasis of the recipes in this chapter is that they are delicious, straightforward to prepare and look so good that guests won't be able to resist them. To enhance the appearance of your buffet food, especially canapés, use attractive dishes and platters – we've collected ours over the years and guests often comment on them. Gone are the days of having matching dishes – the more variety, the better, it seems!

Double Chocolate Clementine Cheesecake *(page 188)*

PLANNING YOUR PARTY

**Here are some tips on perfecting your menu,
whether it is for a drinks party or a buffet:**

Try not to repeat ingredients on the canapés but keep your choices simple.

Try to include as many dishes that can be prepared in advance as possible. They should then
either be ready to serve as is,
or simply need assembling at the last minute.

Make good use of quality convenience foods such as ready-made pastry, roasted peppers,
sauces and meringues.

Cater for those with special diets, especially vegetarians.
Many meat-eaters enjoy vegetarian food too.

Make detailed shopping lists.

Try to include dishes that have contrasting textures, flavours and colours and have a balance
of hot and cold dishes. It's best not to have more than half the savoury canapés as hot ones,
but if you aren't very confident about organising last minute preparations, opt for ones
that can be prepared in advance and then simply reheated (such as the savoury
main courses in this chapter).

It's not necessary to offer a large number of dishes – less is often best. Fewer well-prepared
dishes will often create more of an impact.

Canapés are ideal for a large group of people. Calculating quantities is never easy but a
general guideline is to allow 8–12 canapés per person – two of these should be sweet
ones. As a rule it's best to serve not more than half of the savoury canapés hot.

Do try to enlist the help of guests to hand round food at parties, as it's a good way of
breaking the ice and getting everyone talking and mixing.

QUAIL'S EGGS WITH SEA SALT & CHILLI DIP

You may also like to serve these with a bowl of mayonnaise instead of the spicy dip. **Makes 24** Preparation and cooking time: 25 minutes

12 quail's eggs
125 g (4$\frac{1}{2}$ oz) packet mangetout
salt and freshly ground black pepper
For the dip
1 tablespoon sea salt
1 teaspoon dried crushed red chillies

1 Put the quail's eggs into a pan of cold water and bring to the boil, then simmer for 3 minutes. Drain and put into a bowl of ice-cold water, then remove the shells.
2 Bring a pan of salted water to the boil, add the mangetout, bring back to the boil and cook for 2 minutes. Drain and refresh under cold running water.
3 Mix the dip ingredients together and put them in a small dish.
4   To assemble, cut the eggs in half and wrap a mangetout around each egg securing it with a cocktail stick.
5 Serve the eggs with the dip.

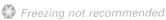 *Freezing recommended*

MEW

CHERRY TOMATOES WITH A SARDINE FILLING

Serves 24 Preparation time: 20 minutes

24 cherry tomatoes, hollowed out
    and well drained
1 x 125 g (4$\frac{1}{2}$ oz) tin boneless
    sardines in olive oil, drained and
    mashed
2.5 cm (1 inch) cucumber, rind
    removed and diced finely
2 teaspoons green peppers, diced
    finely
mayonnaise
salt and a pinch of cayenne pepper
thin slices of lemon cut into
    segments, to garnish

1 Mix the sardines with the cucumber and green peppers, and season with salt and cayenne pepper. Add just enough mayonnaise to bind the mixture together.
2 Pack the mixture into hollowed out tomatoes and garnish with small triangles of fresh lemon, cut from the slices.

Freezing not recommended

Tip: This recipe also makes a very good starter, but for this use a large tomato cut in half.

MEW

RATATOUILLE CROUSTADES

Croustades are so much better than vol-au-vents or sandwiches. As the bases are so crisp and crunchy, few people can believe that they are made from bread. The day I made these, Amy was off school, so we took the bread off-cuts to the canal to feed the ducks – they were very happy! The bases can be made in advance and then stored in an airtight tin. **Makes 24** Preparation time: 30 minutes + cooling (optional) + Cooking time: 15–20 minutes

12 large slices of white bread

175 g (6 oz) butter, melted

1 tablespoon olive oil

1 small onion, chopped finely

1 garlic clove, crushed

1/2 small aubergine, diced

1/2 courgette, diced

1 red pepper, de-seeded and diced

small can of chopped tomatoes

1 teaspoon pesto sauce

salt and freshly ground black pepper

freshly grated Parmesan cheese, to serve

1 Preheat oven to Gas Mark 4/ electric oven 180°C/fan oven 160°C.

2 Remove the crusts from the slices of bread and roll each slice with a rolling pin to flatten. Cut out two 7½ cm (3 inch) rounds from each slice using a pastry cutter.

3 Using tongs, dip each round into the melted butter, shake off any excess and press into patty tins.

4 Bake in the oven for 15–20 minutes until the croustades are crisp and golden brown. Transfer to a wire rack to cool if not using immediately. Otherwise, keep warm until the filling is ready.

5 To make the ratatouille, heat the oil and fry the onion and garlic until soft and transparent. Add the aubergine, courgette and pepper. Cover and cook gently for 10–15 minutes. Add the tomatoes, seasoning and the pesto sauce. Bring back to the boil and simmer, uncovered, until the ratatouille is cooked and reduced.

6 Fill the croustades with the ratatouille and sprinkle with the Parmesan cheese.

 Freezing not recommended

SCC

MUSHROOM CROUSTADES

The mushroom filling is a classic mushroom *duxelles* recipe which creates a smooth paste which has a concentrated mushroom taste. **Makes 24** Preparation and cooking times: 40 minutes and 20 minutes

24 croustades (please see the recipe for Ratatouille Croustades)

15 g ($^{1}/_{2}$ oz) butter

1 small onion, peeled and finely diced

a grating of fresh nutmeg

225 g (8 oz) chestnut mushrooms, sliced

salt and fresh ground black pepper

24 tomato slices, using cherry or baby plum tomatoes

1 Melt the butter in a saucepan and fry the onion for a few minutes.

2 Add the mushrooms and nutmeg and fry until the mushrooms are cooked and the liquid has evaporated. Season with the salt and pepper and blend to a smooth purée – A hand blender does this well.

3 Place a spoonful in each croustades and top with a tomato slice.

 Freezing not recommended

Tip: It's worth making mushroom duxelles just to keep in small batches in the freezer – adding a small amount to casseroles and soups which contain mushrooms, really intensifies the flavour.

SCC

MIRROR BALL

These mirror balls look lovely either hanging on a Christmas tree or in a place where they catch the light, perhaps from a candle or fire. You can use anything as a base as long as it is not too heavy for hanging, but polystyrene or oasis works best. Oasis are available in all sorts of interesting shapes and sizes, especially around Christmas time. Avoid using a shape that is too complicated though, as it will be harder to cover and won't look so good. 'Lills' are available from good haberdashers.

1 Pin each sequin into the polystyrene or oasis shape, overlapping each one a little so you can't see what is underneath.

AG

SALAMI & SUN-DRIED TOMATO BOATS

Serves 12 Preparation time: 10 minutes

50 g (2 oz) cream cheese
3 sun-dried tomatoes, chopped
   finely
12 small slices of Danish salami
12 black olives, stoned

1 Cream together the cheese and tomatoes and spread this mixture over the slices of salami.
2 Place an olive in the centre of each slice of salami and secure it in place with a cocktail stick.

Freezing not recommended

MEW

RAREBIT & MANGO TOASTS

I adore Welsh Rarebit . Here, it's spiced up a little and complemented by the mango chutney. The base is Irish soda bread, so it's a real fusion recipe! The rarebit mixture can be made up to a couple of days in advance and then assembled just before you plan to serve them. **Makes about 25** Preparation time: 15 minutes + 30 minutes chilling

15 g (½ oz) butter

115 g (4 oz) mature Cheddar cheese

1 tablespoon milk

a pinch of cayenne pepper

1 level teaspoon English mustard powder

1 egg yolk

5 slices of soda bread (from the centre of the loaf so that they are the largest and equal in size)

5 teaspoons mango chutney

1 Melt the butter over a gentle heat, add the cheese and stir until it has melted. Add the milk and stir to incorporate it.

2 Remove from the heat and add the cayenne, mustard powder and egg yolk. Mix well. Allow to cool, cover and then refrigerate so that the mixture thickens and sets a little.

3 Heat the grill and toast one side of the soda bread. Turn over and spread the mango chutney over the surface of the untoasted side. Spread the rarebit on top, making sure there is no bread visible. Return to the heat and grill until golden brown.

4 Cut each slice into five equal pieces and serve.

 Freezing not recommended

Tip: On one occasion when I prepared these, I had a few left over – not wanting to waste any, I decided to see how they would be if I reheated them in the oven. I have to say the results were surprisingly good. If you don't want to grill and cut them when your guests are with you, this might be the solution for you!

SCC

TIGER PRAWNS WITH CHILLI MAYONNAISE

Serves 24 Preparation time: 15 minutes + 2 hours marinating + 3–4 minutes cooking

24 shelled raw tiger prawns
1 tablespoon soy sauce
2 tablespoons sweet chilli sauce
1 tablespoon sesame oil
salt and pepper
For the dip
1 tablespoon sweet chilli sauce
2 tablespoons mayonnaise, ready made
2 tablespoons natural yogurt
fresh coriander leaves to garnish

1 Soak wooden cocktail sticks in cold water for 30 minutes (this prevents them from burning during cooking).

2 In a shallow dish combine together the marinade ingredients and add the prawns. Toss well to coat evenly and leave to marinate, covered for about 2 hours.

3 To make the dip mix together the chilli sauce, mayonnaise and yogurt and put into a small dish. Chill until required.

4 Remove prawns from the marinade and thread onto cocktail sticks through the tail and fatter end. Cook either on a preheated grill turning once or fry quickly in a wok or non-stick fry pan for 3–4 minutes.

5 Serve hot with the dip garnished with the chopped coriander leaves.

 Freezing not recommended

Tip: All the preparation can be done well in advance and the prawns cooked quickly at the last minute.

MEW

GOAT'S CHEESE & OLIVE CROSTINI

Crostini are small toasts made from a French stick (ficelle). They make a wonderful base for a variety of toppings. Here they are topped with some Greek ingredients but you could vary them to suit your taste and the available ingredients. **Makes 24** Preparation time: 10 minutes Cooking time: 15 minutes

1 French stick
1 garlic clove
1 soft goat's cheese log
12 Kalamata olives, stoned and
    quartered
12 semi-dried (sunblush) tomatoes
salt and freshly ground black
    pepper

1 Preheat oven to Gas Mark 4/ electric 180°C/fan oven 160°C.
2 Cut the bread on the diagonal, into thin slices. Place on a couple of baking sheets and bake in the oven until they are crisp and golden brown.
3 Rub the garlic over the surface of each slice. Cool the crostini on a wire rack.
4 To assemble, spread the goat's cheese over each slice and season with the salt and pepper. Arrange the olives and tomato pieces attractively on top.

 Freezing not recommended

Tip: The crostini can be made a couple of days in advance and stored in an airtight tin.

SCC

HUMMUS & RED PEPPER CROSTINI

The combination of hummus and sweet pepper is currently a popular one. In this recipe the pepper is roasted but not puréed. You could make your own hummus, but there are so many good quality commercial ones available, it doesn't seem necessary. If you want to cheat further, you could use ready roasted peppers, available in jars or on the deli counter! **Makes 24** Preparation time: 15 minutes Cooking time: 15 minutes

2 red peppers, quartered and
    de-seeded
1 small tub of hummus
24 crostini (see Goat's Cheese and
    Olive Crostini, on this page)
salt and freshly ground black
    pepper
paprika (mild), for sprinkling

1 Preheat the grill to a medium high heat. Place the pepper quarters, skin side up, under the preheated grill and grill until the skins are blackened. Place in a plastic bag, seal and allow to cool.

2 When cool, remove the blackened skin, cut half the pieces into small dice and the other half into strips.

3 Fold the diced pepper into the hummus and season with the salt and pepper. Spread the mixture onto the crostini and use the strips to garnish them. Sprinkle paprika on top.

SCC

CHRISTMAS GAMES WITH GILDED WALNUTS

Christmas may be the only time when we sit down with family and friends to play old-fashioned parlour games or board games.

You will need:
- paper
- pen
- walnuts
- ribbons
- glue
- spray paint
- Christmas tree or bowl with greenery, to display

1 Well in advance, write down questions or forfeits for games such as 'Twenty Questions' or Charades, or indeed any game requiring a forfeit, on small pieces of paper. In fact you could put any mottos, quotes, messages or clues inside these beautiful gilded walnuts to hang on the tree.

2 Carefully crack open the walnuts so that you still have two perfect halves and place the papers inside.

3 If you are going to hang the walnuts on the tree, place a ribbon inside the top before gluing the walnut back together.

4 Now gild your walnut with some spray paint and either hang it on the tree or place it in a bowl with some greenery until required.

AG

MELON WITH PROSCIUTTO HAM

Serves 25–30 Preparation time: 10 minutes **Freezing not recommended**

1 ripe honeydew melon (or use frozen melon balls from the freezer cabinet)
15 slices of Prosciutto ham

1 Cut the melon in half, remove the seeds and scoop out into balls using a melon scoop. Alternatively, cut the melon flesh into cubes.
2 Cut the ham slices in half and fold into concertina shapes.
3 Secure the ham and melon together with cocktail sticks.

MEW

MINI CROISSANTS

Makes 36 Preparation and cooking time: 25 minutes

1 pack of ready-to-bake mini croissant dough
75 g (2³⁄₄ oz) cream cheese (garlic or herbs)
Filling choices for each croissant:
 1 teaspoon finely chopped turkey with ¹⁄₂ teaspoon cranberry sauce
or 15 g (¹⁄₂ oz) Cheddar cheese cut into a rectangles with ¹⁄₂ teaspoon chutney
or 1 cooked cocktail sausage (or spicy sausage such as chorizo) and ¹⁄₄ teaspoon mustard
To glaze
1 egg, beaten
1 tablespoon poppy seeds

1 Preheat oven to Gas Mark 6/ electric oven 200°C/fan oven 180°C.
2 Unroll the croissant dough, roll out thinly and cut through the perforations to make six pieces.
3 Lightly spread each piece with cream cheese and cut into six triangles.
4 Add the filling of choice at the longest side of each triangle and tightly roll up. Form into a crescent shape. Brush with beaten egg and sprinkle with poppy seeds.

5 Cover a baking tray with parchment paper or use a black Teflon sheet. Bake for 8–10 minutes until golden brown.

 Freezing recommended

Freezing: Cool, and then pack into rigid containers before freezing. To use, thaw and reheat in the oven until warmed through.

Tip: You could use ready-to-roll puff pastry instead of the croissant dough. Cut the sheet into 8 cm (3 inch) squares and then divide each square in half diagonally to make triangles. Continue from step 3.

MEW

LEEK & STILTON CRACKERS

Leeks and Stilton go together so well. In this recipe, they are enclosed in crisp filo pastry, shaped into mini crackers and made very festive. **Makes 24** Preparation time: 30 minutes + 20 minutes chilling + Cooking time: 10–15 minutes

1 tablespoon olive oil

2 medium leeks, trimmed and cut into very thin slices

80 g (3 oz) Stilton cheese

12 sheets of filo pastry

50 g (2 oz) butter, melted

salt and freshly ground black pepper

1 Heat the oil in a frying pan and fry the leeks over a moderate heat for a few minutes until they are cooked and very soft. Set aside to cool for about 30 minutes.

2 Preheat oven to Gas Mark 6/ electric oven 200°C/fan oven 180°C.

3 Crumble the cheese into the leeks and season with salt and black pepper.

4 Place a sheet of filo pastry on the work surface, brush with melted butter and cut in half, lengthways. Spoon a little of the leek mixture into the middle of the pastry, at the ends closest to you. Roll up and then pinch both ends to create a cracker.

5 Brush all over with more butter and then place on a large baking sheet, leaving a little gap in between each cracker. Repeat with the remaining mixture.

6 Bake in the oven for 10–15 minutes until crisp and golden brown – if the ends are browning too quickly, you will need to cover them with some foil.

 Freezing not recommended

Tip : You will need to keep the unused sheets of filo pastry covered with some cling film or foil while you are making each cracker, otherwise the pastry will become dry and brittle and unusable.

SCC

SPINACH & BOURSIN POUCHES

It's important to chill the filling before using it because this allows it to thicken. The egg yolk binds the mixture together. Tying chives around the 'neck' of the pouches creates a very professional look! **Makes 24**
Preparation times: 30 minutes + 1 hour chilling + Cooking time: 10–15 minutes

225 g (8 oz) frozen spinach, thawed
fresh nutmeg, grated
125 g packet of Boursin or other
**   cream cheese with garlic and**
**   herbs**
1 egg yolk
50 g (2 oz) butter
9 large sheets of filo pastry
chives, to garnish (optional)

1 Blend the spinach, Boursin, a few gratings of nutmeg and the egg yolk together.

2 Cover and refrigerate for 1 hour.

3 Preheat oven to Gas Mark 6/ electric 200°C/fan oven 180°C.

4 Melt the butter. Brush a sheet of filo pastry with the melted butter and cut it into eight equal squares. Place three squares on top of one another, spoon a teaspoon of the spinach mixture in the centre and bring the four corners together, pinching them together to seal the filling.

5 Brush all over with more butter and place on a large baking sheet.

6 Repeat with the remaining pastry and filling.

7 Bake in the oven for 10–15 minutes.

8 If you are using the chives, tie them around each pouch and serve.

 Freezing recommended

SCC

PARTY PEANUT BUTTER & CHEESE WHIRLS

Makes 20 Preparation and cooking time: 25 minutes

1 sheet of ready-rolled puff pastry
2 tablespoons crunchy peanut
  butter
25 g (1 oz) Cheddar cheese, grated
beaten egg, to glaze

1   Preheat oven to Gas Mark 7/ electric oven 220°C/fan oven 200°C.

2   Spread the pastry with the peanut butter and sprinkle the grated cheese over it.

3   Roll up from each of the long sides of the pastry to the middle to create a whirl-shape. Brush the edges with the beaten egg and press together where they meet. Cut into 20 slices.

4   Line a baking tray with a Teflon sheet or baking parchment. Place each whirl on the tray and brush each with beaten egg.

5   Bake for 8–10 minutes until puffed and golden.

 Freezing recommended

Freezing: These can be stored in the freezer uncooked and baked from frozen as required. Allow a few minutes extra in the oven.
To freeze: Open freeze at the end of stage 3, then pack in a rigid box.

MEW

GRUYÈRE CHEESE PUFFS

Makes approximately 24
Preparation time: 15 minutes
Cooking time: 25 minutes

For the choux pastry
75 g (2³⁄₄ oz) plain flour
¹⁄₄ teaspoon salt
50 g (2 oz) butter
2 eggs, beaten
For the filling
75 g (2³⁄₄ oz) Gruyère cheese,
grated
a pinch of cayenne pepper
oil, for deep-frying

1 Sieve the flour and salt onto a sheet of greaseproof paper.
2 Melt the butter in a small saucepan with 150 ml (¹⁄₄ pint) water, then bring to the boil.
3 Remove the pan from heat, add the flour all at once, then beat the mixture until it forms a paste and leaves the side of the pan clean as it forms a ball.
4 Tip into a mixing bowl and leave to cool until just warm. Using an electric mixer, beat in the eggs a little at a time until it is firm and shiny ('soft peak' – peak top just falls over). Beat in 50 g (2 oz) of the cheese and a pinch of cayenne pepper.
5 Fill a fryer or deep pan one third full of oil and heat to 180°C, or place a bread cube in the oil and if it turns golden brown in 15 seconds, the oil is hot enough. Scoop out a small amount of the cheese mixture with one teaspoon and with another teaspoon on top put carefully into the hot oil.
6 Cook gently in batches until puffed and golden brown, turning with a perforated draining spoon to get an even colour. This takes 7–8 minutes. Drain on a paper kitchen towel.
7 Serve the cheese puffs in a warm dish with the remaining cheese sprinkled over. Watch them disappear!

 Freezing not recommended

Tip: The choux pastry can be made in advance. Once made, cover the surface with oiled cling film and refrigerate until required.

MEW

WHOLE POACHED SALMON

A whole poached salmon is a spectacular dish and makes the perfect centrepiece for a cold buffet. It looks especially colourful surrounded by the Festive Eggs (page 174) and served with the Green Mayonnaise Sauce. This dish is a lighter alternative to counteract all the rich meat and poultry of the festive season and a good choice for the calorie-conscious. If you don't have a fish kettle, use a large roasting tin, cover tightly with foil, and cook as below or place in an oven Gas Mark 4/electric oven 180°C/fan oven 160°C for about 1 hour. **Serves 8** Preparation time: 45 minutes + Cooking time: 15 minutes + Overnight cooling + chilling

1.75 kg (4 lb) fresh whole salmon, gutted
For court bouillon
150 ml (5 fl oz) dry white wine
8 peppercorns
1 small onion, sliced
1 carrot, peeled and sliced
1 bay leaf
2–3 parsley stalks
½ teaspoon salt
1 lime, sliced

To serve
2 limes, sliced finely
Festive Eggs (page 174)
sprigs of dill
Green mayonnaise sauce (page 168)

1 Prepare the salmon. Using the back of a knife, held at an angle, scrape the scales from the whole fish working from the tail to the head. Rinse under cold, running water to remove the scales and all traces of blood from the backbone. Pat the fish dry with kitchen paper.

2 Use a pair of scissors to cut off the salmon's fins from its sides, along its back and belly. Snip the tail into a V shape.

3 Place the salmon on the trivet and lower it into the fish kettle. Pour over the white wine and just enough water to cover, then add the rest of the court bouillon ingredients.

4 Cover and bring the liquid slowly to the boil (approximately 15 minutes). Simmer for 1 minute per 450 g (1 lb) of weight.

5 Turn off the gas or, if using an electric cooker, take the fish kettle off the hot plate.

6 Allow the salmon to cool in its liquor overnight or for several hours. Do not be tempted to lift the lid in the early stages of cooling.

7 Once cold, lift the salmon on the trivet out of the fish kettle and allow it to drain for a few minutes.

8 Lift the fish off the trivet and place it on a large board, flat side uppermost.

9 Using a sharp knife, ease the skin gently away from the flesh and transfer the salmon to a flat serving dish, turning it over. Remove the skin from the other side, but leave the head and tail on for a buffet presentation.

10 Chill the salmon in the refrigerator until ready to serve.

11 Decorate the salmon with slices of lime arranged in an attractive row down the centre of the fish. Place the Festive Eggs around the edge of the platter with sprigs of dill in between.

12 Serve the Green Mayonnaise Sauce separately in a sauceboat.

 *Freezing not recommended*

Tip: To enhance the presentation of the salmon, you could serve it on a sheet of mirror glass or a shiny oval catering plate.

MEW

FESTIVE EGGS

These always look so colourful and attractive. They can be served on their own or to complement a dish such as the Whole Poached Salmon (page 172), where they look pretty served around the edge. **Serves 8–16** Preparation time: 25 minutes + 20 minutes cooking

8 eggs, hard-boiled

For the filling

8 egg yolks

200 g (7 oz) packet of cream cheese

1 tablespoon milk

1 teaspoon sun-dried tomato purée

Suggested garnishes

roll of anchovy fillet with capers

black lumpfish roe

slices of stuffed olive with pimento

baby gherkin sliced into a fan tail

1 Shell the hard-boiled eggs and cut in half, lengthways.

2 Remove the yolks with a teaspoon, add them to the filling ingredients and combine together. Place the egg whites in a bowl of cold water while preparing the filling.

3 Using a 1 cm (½ inch) vegetable rosette piping nozzle in a large piping pastry bag, pipe the filling in a rosette shape into the drained egg whites.

4 To serve, use four halves for each garnish. Chill until required.

 *Freezing not recommended*

MEW

GREEN MAYONNAISE SAUCE

This is a delightful, smooth and tasty sauce, which will complement and enhance a number of cold dishes. It is particularly good when served with the Whole Poached Salmon (page 172), adding colour and interest. It's also good with the Festive Eggs. **Serves 8** Preparation time: 10 minutes + Cooling

200 g (7 oz) cooked and well-drained baby leaf spinach

300 g (10 oz) good quality light mayonnaise

300 g (10 oz) half-fat crème fraîche

salt and freshly ground black pepper

1 Pierce the bag of baby leaf spinach and cook for 4 minutes in a microwave at full power (650 W). Allow it to cool.

2 Remove the spinach from its package and process it, together with the mayonnaise and crème fraîche. Season to taste and put into a sauceboat.

3 Just before serving, grind some black pepper over the top.

 Freezing not recommended

SCC

STILTON AND WALNUT MOUSSES

These little mousses make a pretty and tasty appetiser over the Christmas period. They are delicious served with mixed salad leaves tossed in a cranberry and apple dressing (opposite).

Serves 8 Preparation time: 30 minutes + 2 hours cooling

25 g (1 oz) butter
2 level tablespoons plain flour
200 ml (7 fl oz) each of cold milk and vegetable stock
1 sachet gelatine or vegetarian equivalent
115 g (4 oz) Stilton, crumbled
2 large eggs, separated
150 ml (¼ pint) crème fraîche
50 g (2 oz) walnuts, chopped fairly finely
paprika, to sprinkle

1 Lightly oil and base-line eight ramekin dishes with discs of baking parchment or greased greaseproof paper. Make a sauce by whisking together the butter, flour, milk and stock together over a medium heat until it thickens and begins to boil.

2 Remove from the heat, sprinkle over the gelatine and whisk until dissolved. Add the cheese and stir until melted. Whisk in the egg yolks and season with salt and pepper.

3 Fold in the crème fraîche followed by the egg whites which have been whisked stiffly. Check the seasoning and then spoon the mixture into the prepared dishes. Sprinkle most of the walnuts on top and gently stir into the mousses. Chill until set.

4 Run a knife around the edges and invert onto serving plates. Surround with the mixed salad, which has been tossed in the cranberry dressing, and sprinkle on the reserved walnuts. Sprinkle the tops of the mousses with paprika.

 Freezing not recommended

SCC

CRANBERRY AND APPLE DRESSING

Preparation time: 5 minutes

4 tablespoons cranberry sauce
3 tablespoons olive oil
6 tablespoons apple juice
2 tablespoons red wine vinegar
1 tablespoon lemon juice
1 tablespoon wholegrain mustard
salt and freshly ground black pepper

1 Put all the ingredients in a screw-top jar and shake until well blended. Check the seasoning.

Freezing not recommended

SCC

SHIRT-TIE WRAP
FOR A BOTTLE

This is a fun way to wrap a standard shaped bottle and could be used for any size of bottle, from aftershave to wine.

You could use ordinary wrapping paper – perhaps striped would look more like a shirt, or you could use a page of newspaper such as The Financial Times for a business man or a page from the sports section for a sports enthusiast.

1 To begin, roll the bottle in the paper leaving 2.5 cm (1 inch) extended at the bottom and about 28 cm (11 inches) at the top. Fold the paper onto the bottom and tape in place. Fold about 20 cm (8 inches) over at the top, towards the back of the bottle and tape this in place. Now fold the remaining 7 cm (3 inches) in half, towards the front, and staple it in the middle. You should now have a flat piece of paper about 4 cm (1½ inches) wide.

2 Make a 5 cm (2 inch) cut along this paper, just under the folded edge, each side of the neck of the bottle, and fold it towards the back to make the shoulders, then stick it down. Open the flat piece to form a tube, or collar.

3 Thread a piece of 2.5 cm (1 inch) wide fabric or ribbon through to make the tie. Tape it securely inside the tube at both ends. Gently pull these two ends together towards the front and knot the tie.

AG

TURKEY CHILLI

This is one of those quick and easy one-pot dishes that is ideal for trouble-free entertaining. Serve it with some plain, boiled rice and a green salad. **Serves 8** Preparation time: 20 minutes + Cooking time: 45 minutes cooking

225 g (8 oz) medium onions, chopped roughly

2 tablespoons oil

4 tablespoons plain flour

2 teaspoons chilli flakes for mild flavour or 1 tablespoon chilli flakes for hot flavour

400 g can of chopped tomatoes

2 tablespoons Worcestershire sauce

4 tablespoons tomato purée

850 ml (1½ pints) turkey stock

1 tablespoon caster sugar

2–3 bay leaves

700 g (1 lb 9 oz) cooked turkey meat, cut into fork-size pieces

450 g (1 lb) jar of roasted red peppers, drained and diced

425 g can of red kidney beans in chilli sauce

salt and freshly ground black pepper

fresh coriander leaves, chopped, to garnish

1 Heat the oil in a large heavy-based casserole dish and sauté the onions until soft. Stir in the flour and chilli seasoning and cook gently for 2 minutes.

2 Add the tomatoes, Worcestershire sauce, tomato purée, stock, sugar, bay leaves and seasoning. Bring to the boil, stirring all the time, then simmer, covered, for 30 minutes.

3 Stir in the turkey, peppers and beans. Simmer for a further 10 minutes.

4 Remove the bay leaves before serving and garnish with coriander leaves.

 Freezing not recommended

MEW

ITALIAN PLAIT

This will look so impressive on your buffet table – the plait looks difficult but is very straightforward. The colours look so attractive when you cut it into slices and the asparagus spears add a touch of luxury as well as complementing the other ingredients. It can be made in advance and then baked (from step 10) just before you need it. Although it is intended to be served hot, it is also delicious cold. **Serves 6–8** Preparation time: 40 minutes + 30 minutes cooling Cooking time: 30–40 minutes

1 aubergine, cut into 1 cm (1/2 inch) cubes
1 red onion, peeled and cut into pieces the same size as the aubergine
225 g (8 oz) chestnut mushrooms, wiped with kitchen paper and halved
5 midi plum tomatoes, halved
2 red peppers, halved, de-seeded and cut into 1 cm (1/2 inch) pieces
2 garlic cloves, peeled and crushed
2 sprigs of fresh thyme, leaves removed, or 1 teaspoon dried thyme
3 tablespoons extra virgin olive oil
125 g (4 1/2 oz) thin asparagus spears
500 g (1 lb 2 oz) puff pastry
250 g tub of ricotta cheese

60 g (2 1/2 oz) grated Parmesan
50 g (2 oz) pine nuts, toasted lightly
1 egg, beaten
salt and freshly ground black pepper
To serve
roasted midi plum tomatoes
a few rocket leaves

1 Preheat oven to Gas Mark 6/ electric oven 200°C/fan oven 180°C.
2 Place the first seven ingredients in a single layer in roasting tins – you will probably need two. Sprinkle over the oil and mix in thoroughly so that the vegetables are coated evenly. Season with salt and pepper.
3 Roast in the oven for about 30 minutes until the vegetables are tender and beginning to turn brown. Remove from the oven and allow to cool for about half an hour.
4 In the meantime, steam the asparagus tips until they are just tender and rinse under cold water to prevent them from cooking further.
5 Reduce the oven temperature to Gas Mark 5/electric oven 190°C/fan oven 170°C.
6 Reserve a small piece of the pastry and set aside. Roll the rest of it out to a large rectangle of about 25 x 30 cm (10 x 12 inches).
7 Spoon the roasted vegetables down the centre of the pastry, to a width of about 13 cm (5 inches). Dot the ricotta all over, sprinkle over

the Parmesan cheese and pine nuts and then lay the asparagus spears over the cheeses.
8 Using the tip of a sharp knife, cut the pastry diagonally on either side of the vegetables leaving about 2 1/2 cm (1 inch) between each. Lift the end pieces over the filling and then the strips, alternating from each side and brushing with the beaten egg. You need to ensure that the filling is completely enclosed – to do this simply push in the sides and lift up the strips a little higher.
9 Roll out the reserved pastry and cut it into holly leaf shapes or cut into 3 strips and create a plait. Brush with the egg and arrange the pastry leaves or plait along the centre where the strips meet.
10 Bake in the oven for 30–40 minutes – you will probably need to cover the top loosely with foil to prevent it from getting too brown towards the end of the cooking time.
11 Transfer to a serving platter and cut one slice to reveal the filling. Garnish with the roasted tomatoes and some salad leaves such as rocket, if you wish.

❄ *Freezing recommended*

Freezing: Open-freeze the plait on a tray and then place in a freezer bag. Thaw overnight in the fridge and then warm through in a moderate oven.

FRUITY PORK WITH GINGER

This is one 'cook ahead' dish that everyone will want to copy. The real fruity flavour combined with the spices makes this pork dish a firm favourite. It is delicious with rice. **Serves 8**
Preparation time: 30 minutes + overnight soaking + Cooking time: 1½–2 hours

125 g (4½ oz) dried apricots, soaked overnight in ginger ale
600 ml (1 pint) ginger ale
5 tablespoons oil
1 kg (2 lb 4 oz) shoulder of pork, cut into 2.5 cm (1 inch) cubes, or diced pork
2 medium onions, chopped roughly
2 garlic cloves, crushed
50 g (2 oz) plain flour
2 tablespoons Madras spice blend
300 ml (½ pint) stock
125 ml (4½ fl oz) freshly squeezed orange juice
1 tablespoon unrefined dark muscovado sugar
125 g (4½ oz) sultanas
2 bay leaves
2.5 cm (1 inch) piece of fresh root ginger, peeled and grated
100 g (3½ oz) okra, trimmed
50 g (2 oz) cashew nuts, (optional)
salt and freshly ground black pepper
1 tablespoon chopped coriander, to serve

1 Preheat oven to Gas Mark 3/ electric oven 160°C/fan oven 140°C.
2 Strain the apricots from the ginger ale and retain the liquid.
3 Heat 4 tablespoons of oil in a large deep frying pan and, over a high heat, quickly sauté the pork in batches to seal in the juices and brown it. Use a draining spoon to transfer the pork to an ovenproof casserole dish.
4 Add the remaining 1 tablespoon of oil to the pork sediment left in the frying pan and fry the onions and garlic gently until soft. Mix in the flour and Madras spice blend and cook for 2–3 minutes, stirring frequently.
5 Gradually pour over the stock, reserved ginger ale and orange juice, stirring all the time. Add the sugar and bring slowly to the boil (continue stirring). You should find the base of the frying pan is now free of pork residue. Season with salt and pepper, then add the apricots, sultanas, bay leaves and ginger.
6 Put into the casserole dish with the pork and stir well to combine the ingredients. Cover and cook in the oven for 1½–2 hours or until the pork is tender. Add the okra for the last 10 minutes of cooking time.
7 Remove the bay leaves and stir in the cashew nuts, if using.

8 Serve the pork casserole garnished with the chopped coriander

 Freezing recommended

Tip: This can be made the day before and, after cooling, stored in a refrigerator to allow the flavours to develop.

MEW

AROMATIC PILAFF RICE

This is such a versatile recipe. It goes perfectly with the Fruity Pork with Ginger (page 180), but is also good served with grilled meats such as chicken. Alternatively, stir-fry some prawns or vegetables and mix them in to make a really tasty buffet dish. **Serves 8**
Preparation time: 20 minutes +
Cooking time: 25 minutes

1 tablespoon olive oil

1 small onion, chopped finely

1 garlic clove, crushed

225 g (8 oz) long grain rice, preferably basmati

2.5 cm (1 inch) piece of fresh root ginger, peeled and freshly grated

½ teaspoon turmeric

1 cinnamon stick, approximately 8 cm (3¼ inches) long

3 cloves

1 tablespoon unrefined light muscovado sugar

425 ml (15 fl oz) stock

25 g (1 oz) butter

75 g (2¾ oz) shelled nuts, e.g. pistachios, almonds or cashews

salt and freshly ground black pepper

1 Preheat oven to Gas Mark 3/ electric oven 160°C/fan oven 140°C.

2 Heat the oil in a flameproof casserole dish, add the onions and garlic and cook gently for 2–3 minutes until translucent.

3 Add the rice and cook gently, without allowing colouring, for 2–3 minutes.

4 Stir in the ginger, turmeric, cinnamon, cloves and sugar.

5 Pour over the stock and bring slowly to the boil, stirring occasionally. Season.

6 Cover the pilaff and place in the oven for approximately 15–20 minutes or until the rice is tender and all the stock has been absorbed.

7 Dot knobs of butter over the surface of the rice and stir in with the nuts with a fork.

 Freezing not recommended

Tip: If serving with Fruity Pork and Ginger (page 180), add the segments of one orange to the finished dish.

Tips for cooking rice:
1. Do not stir during cooking as this releases starch, making the grains stick together.
2. To test if the rice is cooked, lift a grain out of the dish and bite on the grain. It should be firm but not crunchy.
3. Allow 50 g (2 oz) raw weight of rice per person.

MEW

SWEET PEPPER PASTA SALAD

This colourful salad can be served either warm or cold. Here I have used a ready-made red pepper tapenade, which I think complements the other ingredients well, but you could use a traditional tapenade instead. The mozzarella can be replaced with feta cheese.

Serves 8 Preparation time: 30 minutes

**4 large red peppers, quartered and
    de-seeded**

**450 g (1 lb) dried pasta shapes,such
    as fusili or shells**

**90 g pot of sweet red pepper
    tapenade**

**100 g (3½ oz) Kalamata olives,
    stoned and cut into slivers**

**125 g ball of mozzarella, drained
    and diced**

**salt and freshly ground black
    pepper**

a handful of fresh basil leaves, torn

1 Grill the peppers until the skins have blackened. Place them in a plastic bag and seal.

2 In a large pan, cook the pasta according to the packet instructions.

3 Remove the peppers from the plastic bag, peel away the skin and cut into strips.

4 Drain the pasta and return it to the pan. Stir in the tapenade, followed by the pepper strips, olives, mozzarella and seasoning.

5 Transfer the salad to a large serving bowl.

6 Just before serving, stir in the basil leaves.

 Freezing not recommended

SCC

MINI CARAMEL & CHOCOLATE MERINGUES

Meringues are usually a popular dessert option and so I thought it would be a good idea to create a mini version as a sweet canapé. The contrast of the chocolate and caramel works well in terms of both taste and appearance. The meringues, undecorated, can be made well in advance, stored in an airtight tin, and then simply finished on the day of your party. **Makes 20** Preparation time: 45 minutes + cooling 1 hour + Cooking time: 1–1½ hours

3 egg whites
80 g (3 oz) caster sugar
80 g 3 oz) light muscovado sugar
150 g (5 oz) plain chocolate, melted
150 ml (¼ pint) double cream

1 Preheat oven to Gas Mark ½/ electric 120°C/fan oven 100°C.

2 Line two baking trays with parchment paper.

3 Place the egg whites in a large bowl and whisk on high/top speed until stiff but not dry. Combine the two sugars and make sure that there are no lumps. Add the sugars to the egg whites, a teaspoon at a time, while whisking on high speed, until all the sugar has been incorporated.

4 Spoon the meringue into a large piping bag with a nozzle 1 cm (½ inch). Pipe small shells (either 'blob' or 'coil') onto the parchment paper, leaving a gap between each one. If you don't feel confident enough to pipe, simply spoon small shells, using two dessert spoons, onto the parchment paper.

5 Bake in the oven for about 1–1½ hours. When they are cooked, they will lift easily from the paper and sound hollow when tapped underneath. Turn off the oven and leave to cool in the oven with the door left ajar.

6 Place a large piece of greaseproof paper on the work surface. Dip the flat underside of each meringue into the melted chocolate, shake off any excess and then carefully place on the paper with the chocolate surface facing upwards. Repeat with the remaining meringue shells. Leave to set.

7 Whip the cream until it is fairly stiff, taking care not to over-whip. Using a small palette knife, spread a little cream onto the chocolate surfaces of half the meringues and then sandwich with the remaining meringue shells. Chill until ready to serve.

Freezing not recommended

SCC

CHERRY & WHITE CHOCOLATE SHORTBREAD

These little shortbread canapés look pretty and the contrasting flavours and textures work well together. Soaking the cherries in kirsch gives them a bit of a 'kick'! The shortbreads can be made a few days in advance and stored in an airtight tin.
Makes 36 Preparation time: 30 minutes + Cooking time: 20 minutes

18 black cherries, stoned and halved
Kirsch
115 g (4 oz) butter
50 g (2 oz) caster sugar
115 g (4 oz) plain flour
40 g (1½ oz) cornflour
80 g (3 oz) white chocolate, broken into squares
200 g carton of cream cheese

1 Preheat the oven to Gas Mark 3/ electric 160°C/fan oven 140°C.
2 Grease a large baking sheet, or line with baking parchment. Place the cherries in a bowl and cover with kirsch.
3 Place the butter and sugar in a bowl. Cream together until soft.
4 Combine the flour and cornflour and add to the creamed butter in stages, adding more once the previous amount has been worked in.
5 Knead together and then roll out on a floured work surface to a thickness of 8 mm (³⁄8 inch). Cut out circles using a 3 cm (1¼ inch) cutter. You will need to re-roll pieces to make the required number.
6 Bake in the oven for 15–20 minutes until the shortbread is pale golden brown in colour and firm to the touch. Transfer to a wire rack and leave to cool.
7 Set a bowl over a pan of barely simmering water and melt the chocolate in it. Allow it to cool and then mix it with the cream cheese in a bowl.
8 Place the mixture in a piping bag fitted with a star nozzle. Pipe rosettes in the centre of each biscuit or if you don't feel confident enough to pipe the chocolate cream, simply spoon it neatly into the centre using a teaspoon.
9 Just before serving, place the cherry halves on kitchen paper to prevent any excess juices discolouring. Place a half cherry, cut side down, on top of the chocolate cream.

 Freezing not recommended

SCC

MANGO DATES

Dates make a wonderful container for fillings if you cut a slit in them and remove the stones. Here they are filled with a creamy mango mixture, which tastes exotic and also looks pretty. You will need to use a piping bag to fill them neatly. Do use fresh dates – their flavour is far superior. **Makes 24** Preparation time: 20 minutes

24 fresh dates
1 medium size, ripe mango
200 g carton of cream cheese (not the low-fat variety)
hazelnuts, roasted and chopped

1 Cut a slit in the top of each date and carefully remove the stone. Gently press the sides apart to create an opening for the filling.
2 Peel the mango and remove the stone. Purée the flesh and then blend with the cream cheese.
3 Spoon the mango cream into a piping bag fitted with a star nozzle, then pipe it into the 'hole' in the dates.
4 Sprinkle the hazelnuts on top.

 Freezing not recommended

SCC

ORANGE CHOCOLATE TRUFFLES

These little truffles make a welcome gift at Christmas. They are flavoured with orange by using 'Maya Gold', organic dark chocolate and Cointreau . You can adapt the flavour with the appropriate liqueur and/or chocolate. The cake crumbs bind the mixture together and make it more manageable. I used cocoa powder to coat the truffles but you could use grated chocolate and/or chopped nuts. As the truffles contain fresh cream, they should be kept in the fridge. They also freeze beautifully and can be eaten straight from the freezer! *Makes 40* Preparation time: 10 minutes + Cooling + 4 hours chilling

150 g (5 oz) Maya Gold chocolate
150 ml (¼ pint) double cream
50 g (2 oz) unsalted butter
200 g (7 oz) Madeira cake
2 tablespoons Cointreau or Grand Marnier
cocoa powder, sifted, for coating

1 Place the chocolate, cream and butter in a saucepan and melt over a very gentle heat (this will ensure a good texture and flavour). Remove from the heat and cool.

2 Break the cake into fine crumbs – it's easy in a food processor. Add the crumbs to the melted chocolate, together with the alcohol, mix well and allow to cool.

3 When the mixture is cool, place it in the fridge for about 4 hours until it is firm.

4 Remove from the fridge and leave it at room temperature for about 15 minutes to soften slightly.

5 Using a parisienne/melon baller, scoop out a ball of the truffle mixture, roll in your hand to form an even ball and then toss in sifted cocoa powder. Place the truffles on a sheet of greaseproof paper and continue making the rest in the same way.

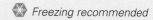 *Freezing recommended*

Freezing: Open freeze on a large tray. When frozen, pack in a freezer bag and tie.

To thaw, simply place on a serving dish and allow to thaw at room temperature for a few minutes.

Tip: Wear latex gloves when rolling the truffles into balls – it's less messy and helps prevent the warmth from your hands affecting the texture of the chocolate.

SCC

STOLLEN BREAD & BUTTER PUDDING

This is a richer and, I think you will agree, a far tastier alternative to the traditional version of bread and butter pudding: Stollen is a German-style fruit cake made with marzipan, fruits and butter and all these delicious flavours permeate the rich vanilla custard. I've added Amaretto liqueur to complement the marzipan but you could use brandy. **Serves 8** Preparation time: 30 minutes + standing 1 hour + Cooking time: 40–45 minutes

150 ml (¼ pint) double cream
425 ml (¾ pint) milk
1 vanilla pod
50 g (2 oz) muscovado sugar
4 eggs, beaten
1 tablespoon Amaretto liqueur
1teaspoon ground cinnamon
14 thin slices of stollen (page 28)
   or shop-bought
50 g (2 oz) butter, softened, plus
   some extra for greasing

1 Place the cream and milk in a saucepan. Using the tip of a sharp knife, split the vanilla pod down its length, scrape out the seeds and add the pod and seeds to the cream mixture. Bring to just below the boil, slowly, remove from the heat and leave to infuse for 10 minutes.

2 Whisk the eggs and sugar together then add the cream mixture, while continuing to whisk. Add the Amaretto and half the cinnamon.

3 Spread the stollen slices on one side with the butter and then butter an ovenproof dish (the one I used was 21 x 31cm (8 x 12 inches). Arrange the slices in the dish, making sure that they overlap slightly.

4 Strain the custard over the slices, sprinkle with the remaining cinnamon and cover with cling film.

5 Leave to soak for 1 hour or place in the fridge and leave for up to two days until ready to bake – if you place it in the fridge, it's best to bring it to room temperature before baking.

6 Preheat oven to Gas Mark 4/ electric oven 180°C/fan oven 160°C. Bake for 40–45 minutes until the top is firm to the touch and golden. Serve with lashings of hot custard, preferably with the addition of Amaretto or brandy!

Freezing not recommended

SCC

DOUBLE CHOCOLATE CLEMENTINE CHEESECAKE

A cheesecake is always a good option for a buffet as most people like them and they cut well. This one combines dark and white chocolate and puréed clementines, swirled together, so it looks really impressive and requires no further decoration once cooked. **Serves 10–12**
Preparation time: 30 minutes
Cooking time: 1 hour 30 minutes
+ 2 hours chilling

350 g (12 oz) **clementines, peeled**
50 g (2 oz) **caster sugar**
80 g (3 oz) **butter**
1 tablespoon **cocoa powder**
150 g (5 oz) **digestive biscuits, crushed**
80 g (3 oz) **amaretti biscuits, crushed**
300 ml (½ pint) **single cream**
115 g (4 oz) **each of white and plain chocolate**
2 x 250 g **tubs ricotta cheese**
4 **eggs**
80 g (3 oz) **light muscovado sugar**

1 Wash the clementines, place them in a saucepan and cover with water. Bring to the boil and simmer for 25 minutes until tender. Drain the clementines, cool a little and liquidise with the caster sugar. Set aside.

2 Preheat oven to Gas Mark 2/ electric oven 150°C/fan oven 130°C.

3 Melt the butter in a saucepan, and stir in the cocoa powder. Remove from the heat and add the biscuits.

4 Spoon into a greased 25 cm (10 inch) springform tin. Press down (a potato masher does this well) and place in the fridge to set.

5 Place the two chocolates in separate saucepans. Divide the cream between the pans and melt the chocolate mixtures over a gentle heat. Set aside to cool.

6 Divide the clementine purée, ricotta cheese, eggs and muscovado sugar between two bowls and mix well. Beat in the melted chocolates.

7 Pour the dark chocolate mixture onto the base and then pour the white chocolate mixture into the centre of the dark chocolate mixture. Using a skewer or something similar, swirl the two mixtures together.

8 Bake in the oven for about 1½ hours until it has set. Switch off the oven and allow the cheesecake to cool in the oven with the door open. Chill in the fridge for at least 2 hours.

9 To serve, remove the cheesecake from the tin and place on a serving plate. Allow it to come to room temperature. If using, serve with whipped cream and decorate with clementine zest.

 *Freezing recommended*

Freezing: To freeze, open-freeze the cheesecake on the tin base, remove the base and place in a freezer bag. Thaw overnight in the fridge on the serving plate.

SCC

BLACK FOREST & WHITE CHOCOLATE CHEESE RING

This is a worthy dessert for a buffet as the contrast in the two tiers looks spectacular – one is full of dark, coloured fruits set in jelly and the other is a creamy white mousse. It does take a bit of time to make but it can be prepared well in advance. The appreciative comments from your guests will make the effort worthwhile. If you don't have a plastic ring mould (the fruits will react against a metal mould) or you're not confident about turning it out, you could make the dessert in a loaf tin, lightly oiled and lined with cling film.

Serves 8 Preparation time: 40 minutes + 4–6 hours chilling

500 g packet of frozen Black Forest Fruits (or similar), thawed and drained

100 g (3½ oz) caster sugar

2 sachets of gelatine

100 g (3½ oz) white chocolate, broken into pieces

2 x 200 g tubs of cream cheese

150 ml (¼ pint) double cream, whipped to soft peaks

1 Place the thawed, drained fruits in a saucepan with 150 ml (¼ pint) water and half the sugar.

2 Bring to the boil over a moderate heat and simmer for just a minute.

3 Remove from the heat and sprinkle a sachet of gelatine over the fruit. Stir carefully with a wooden spoon, so as not to damage the fruit, until the gelatine has dissolved (when you look at the liquid in a large spoon, there should be no crystals visible).

4 Spoon the mixture into the chosen mould, which should have a capacity of 1.2 litres (2 pints). When cold, place the ring in the fridge to set.

5 Sprinkle the second sachet of gelatine over 3 tablespoons of cold water in a small bowl and leave for a couple of minutes to go spongy. Dissolve by setting the bowl in a pan of hot water and stirring. Alternatively, you could heat the mixture in a microwave for 30 seconds on full power. Set aside to cool.

6 Melt the white chocolate in a bowl, set it over a pan of hot water and leave it to melt. Stir it and set aside to cool.

7 Place the cream cheese in a bowl with the remaining sugar. Mix well and then stir in the melted white chocolate followed by the gelatine. Mix thoroughly.

8 Fold in the whipped cream. Spoon it over the set fruits and chill until set.

9 To serve, dip the ring mould in a bowl of hot water for a short while, dip a small palette knife in hot water and use it to ease the filling away from the sides and then check to see if the mixture is loose enough to turn out. You may need to dip it in the hot water again. When you think it's ready, place a serving platter on top of the mould and invert it – the mousse should 'drop' onto the platter. If it doesn't, you could rub a hot dishcloth around the mould to ease the mousse out of the mould. If you've used a loaf tin, simply invert it on to the serving platter and peel away the cling film.

 Freezing not recommended

Tip: It's a good idea to wet the serving platter – this enables you to move the dessert if it isn't quite central or in the position in which you want it to be.

SCC

RASPBERRY MOUSSE PAVLOVA GATEAU

Hazelnuts and raspberries have a natural affinity – combining them in this way creates a stunning and mouth-watering dessert. I have to admit that this is a time-consuming dessert but I hope you will agree it is well worth the effort. The pavlova can be made in advance and stored in an airtight container.

Serves 8 Preparation time: 1 hour Cooking time: 30–40 minutes Cooling time: 1 hour

For the pavlova

100 g (3½ oz) hazelnuts, ground

4 egg whites

225 g (8 oz) caster sugar

1 teaspoon white wine vinegar

1 teaspoon vanilla extract

1 teaspoon cornflour

For the raspberry mousse

175 g (6 oz) fresh raspberries (you can use frozen ones that have thawed)

1 sachet of gelatine powder

200 g carton of cream cheese

50 g (2 oz) caster sugar

150 ml (¼ pint) double cream, whisked to soft peaks

For the topping

300 ml (½ pint) whipping cream, whipped

about 12 whole hazelnuts

115 g (4 oz) fresh raspberries

1 Preheat oven to Gas Mark 5/ electric oven 190°C/fan oven 170°C.

2 Place the ground hazelnuts in a layer on a baking sheet and bake in the oven for about 10 minutes or until they become golden in colour. Allow to cool.

3 Lightly oil three 20 cm (8 inch) loose-bottomed sandwich tins. Base-line with baking parchment paper (see Tips). Meanwhile, whisk the egg whites in a large bowl at a high speed until they are stiff. Add the sugar, a teaspoon at a time, while continuing to whisk at a high speed.

4 Place the cornflour, vanilla extract and white wine vinegar in a small dish and mix to form a smooth paste. Fold this mixture into the meringue, followed by the baked hazelnuts, taking care not to knock out any of the air.

5 Divide the meringue between the three prepared tins. Level the surface. Bake in the oven for 30–40 minutes until it is crisp and golden (it will be like marshmallow on the inside).

6 Run a knife around the edge of the meringue to ensure it hasn't stuck to the tin, remove from the tin, peel away the parchment paper and cool on wire racks.

7 In the meantime, make the raspberry mousse. Purée the raspberries and pass them through a sieve, ideally a nylon one.

8 Sprinkle the gelatine onto 3 tablespoons of cold water. Leave for a few minutes and then dissolve by placing the dish in a bowl of hot water, or microwave on High for 30 seconds. Stir until there are no granules visible and allow to cool.

9 Place the cream cheese, raspberry purée and caster sugar in a bowl and whisk together to combine. Pour in the dissolved gelatine and whisk again to combine. Fold in the whipped cream. Leave for a few minutes, by which time the mixture will have started to set.

10 Place one of the meringue discs, flat side down, in a 20 cm (8 inch) loose-bottomed or springform cake tin. Spoon half the mousse on top and level the surface. Place a second disc on top and press gently. Add the remaining mousse and place the third disc, flat side up, on top. Once again, press down gently. Place in the fridge for at least 1 hour to set.

11 Remove the gâteau from the cake tin and carefully transfer it to a serving plate. Spoon two thirds of the whipped cream on top and spread evenly over the surface. Spoon the remaining cream into a piping bag fitted with a star nozzle and pipe rosettes around the edge of the meringue. Place a hazelnut on top of each rosette and arrange the raspberries in the centre.

 *Freezing recommended*

Freezing: Open freeze at the end of stage 11 and wrap in a freezer bag. Thaw the gateau on the serving plate overnight in the fridge.

Tips: Lakeland sell baking parchment circles of different diameters.

Whether freezing or not, it's best to place the raspberries on a few sheets of kitchen paper to remove any excess juice.

SNOWGLOBE

Children love to play with snow globes and will be thrilled to make one of their own and to see the glitter falling on the little figures.

You will need:
- a small jar with a flat top
- glitter
- glycerine
- cake decorations such as a snowman, pine trees or a Father Christmas
- some superglue

(make sure that the decorations are small enough to stand up inside the jar)

1 Superglue the decorations to the inside of the lid, leaving enough room around the edge for the lid to screw back on to the jar.

2 Add a couple of teaspoons of glitter. The glycerine is not essential, but it will stop the glitter from forming clumps.

3 Now screw the lid onto the jar very tightly. You may want to superglue the lid in place too (don't let young children play with or use superglue).

4 Give the jar a shake and turn it over to watch the snow falling on the snow scene.

AG

Christmas
Drinks

When you have friends and family around over Christmas, it's a good chance to offer some interesting drinks instead of the usual wine, beer, mineral water and fruit juice. Many purists claim that you shouldn't 'mess around' with drinks. But for special occasions it's fun to mix your own drinks – they'll make your parties even more enjoyable and your guests will appreciate the trouble you have taken. Who can resist a glass of mulled wine on a cold winter's day when they smell the wonderful spicy aroma? In this chapter, there are drinks to suit all tastes and ages as well as some non-alcoholic drinks for drivers. The difficulty will be deciding which ones to make!

Mulled Red Wine *(page 199)*

ICE PILLAR TABLE DECORATION

For this unusual table decoration you will need:
- a pillar candle
- an empty milk or juice carton or something similar (try to find something with a flat bottom as it will be more stable)
- some greenery, such as sprigs of holly or foliage, or flowers plus extra for display
- enough space in the freezer to accommodate the arrangement while it freezes. If you like, you can make coloured ice by adding some food colouring to the water.

1 Centre your candle in the carton and cut the top down so that it is well below the top of the candle.
2 Arrange the greenery and flowers around the candle and fill with water, up to about 5 cm (2 inches) below the top of the carton. Ensure that the foliage doesn't overhang the candle in case it catches fire.
3 Freeze the carton until the ice has set – this is best done overnight.

4 To remove the carton, run it briefly under a hot tap and peel away. Keep the arrangement frozen until it is required – you could use a cold box if you are short of freezer space, or even keep the ice decoration outside if the the temperature is freezing.
5 To display your ice pillar, place it in a shallow dish. You may want to arrange some additional foliage around the bottom.

For an alternative ice decoration, you will need:
- a shallow dish
- a few yoghurt pots
- pebbles
- tea lights

1 Fill a shallow dish with water.
2 When the water is frozen, place a few yoghurt pots weighed down with pebbles on top of the ice, fill the dish with more water and refreeze.
3 When it is frozen remove the yoghurt pots (you may need to add some warm water to loosen them).
4 Place tea lights in the spaces left and put the decoration in a shallow dish so that as the ice begins to melt, it will be contained in the dish.

Christmas Tip: If you put any candle on top of a mirror, the light will be reflected and it will appear to glow more brightly. If you can't find a suitable mirror you could use an old CD.

AG

CHRISTMAS CIDER PUNCH

This will certainly warm the spirit, but do warn drivers that this packs quite a punch! **Serves 8** Preparation and cooking time: 20 minutes + 15 minutes infusing

8 sugar cubes

2 large oranges

8 cloves

1 cinnamon stick

½ teaspoon grated nutmeg

pared rind and juice of 2 lemons

2 litres (3½ pints) dry cider

150 ml (¼ pint) brandy

1 Rub the sugar cubes over the oranges to absorb the zest.

2 Cut the oranges in half, squeeze the juice from them and put into a saucepan with the sugar cubes. Add the spices and 150 ml (¼ pint) water and stir. Leave to infuse for 15 minutes.

3 Add the lemon rind and juice. Heat gently until the sugar dissolves, then add the cider and continue to heat until hot.

4 Serve in glass punch cups if you have them.

 Freezing not recommended

Tip: To prevent glassware from cracking, stand a teaspoon in the cups before pouring in the hot liquid.

MEW

SPICY FRUIT CUP

This is a delicious and festive non-alcoholic drink. It's ideal for children, any guests who are driving or for those who prefer not to drink alcohol. **Serves 10** Preparation time: 10 minutes

assorted chopped fruit (2 red apples, 1 small pineapple, 2 oranges)

500 ml (18 fl oz) orange juice or pineapple juice

1 litre (1¾ pints) clear apple juice

a dash of Ribena

½ teaspoon mixed spice

2 litres (3½ pints) fresh lemonade, chilled in refrigerator

a few ice cubes

a few sprigs of mint, to decorate

1 Place the fruit in a punch bowl or large glass bowl.

2 Mix together the juices, Ribena and spice. Pour over the fruit.

3 Add the chilled lemonade, ice cubes and mint sprigs just before serving.

 *Freezing not recommended*

MEW

ICED CHOCOLATE & BANANA SMOOTHIE

This is a meal in a glass. Smoothies are nutritious, being a blend of yogurt, milk or juice, as well as delicious and easy to make. **Serves 4** Preparation time: 5 minutes + chilling

600 ml (1 pint) cold fresh milk

2–3 tablespoons drinking chocolate

150 ml (¼ pint) natural yogurt

1 banana, mashed or frozen pieces
   of 1 banana (see Tip)

2 tablespoons rum (optional)

To serve

1 teaspoon drinking chocolate

4 pink marshmallows, toasted

1 Put all the ingredients, except those for serving, into a blender and liquidise until smooth.

2 Pour into individual glasses, and chill in the fridge. To serve, top each chilled smoothie with a toasted marshmallow and a dusting of drinking chocolate.

 Freezing not recommended

Tip: Bananas freeze well. Chop them into smaller pieces and use straight from the freezer.

   For a richer, creamier taste, use Greek yogurt instead of natural yogurt or, if you're counting calories, low fat yogurt.

MEW

SWEET-SCENTED POMANDER

This may be an old-fashioned idea, but it is still worth using over and over again as the scent is wonderful and lasts for months. If you have made pomanders before with oranges, why not try using lemons or limes? Another variation is to include bay leaves (see below).

You will need:

- an unblemished citrus fruit
- 2 pieces of 1 cm (1/2 inch) wide ribbon
- needle
- cloves
- ribbon loop and bow
- tassel (optional)

1 Starting at the top of the citrus fruit, take a 1 cm (1/2 inch) wide piece of ribbon and pin it directly into the fruit. Take the ribbon around the fruit lengthways and pin it again at the top. Do the same thing with another piece of ribbon, running at a 45 degree angle to the first.

2 Now make a hole anywhere in the fruit with a needle and push a clove into the hole. Cover the fruit completely with cloves.

3 Pin a ribbon loop and bow on top of the fruit for hanging and add a tassel on the bottom if you like.

4 To attach bay leaves, lay the leaf vertically down the side of the fruit and, beginning with the widest part of the leaf, insert the stem of the clove into the fruit just next to the bay leaf, but not through it. The head of the clove should hold the leaf in place but not pierce it. Insert cloves all the way around the leaf.

AG

MULLED RED WINE (GLÜHWEIN)

A small glass of this warm, spicy red wine will revive you after a brisk walk in the crisp winter air or a bout of Christmas shopping.
Serves 8–10 Preparation time: 20 minutes

2 litres (3 1/2 pints) red wine

3 cinnamon sticks

1 fresh orange, sliced

1 fresh lemon, sliced

8 whole cloves

75 g (2 3/4 oz) caster sugar

1 Place all the ingredients in a large pan. Stir over a low heat for 20 minutes. Do not allow to boil.

2 Serve warm.

 Freezing not recommended

Tip: If making in bulk, use a good quality box of wine.

MEW

THANK YOU POSTCARDS

Making individual postcards is a good way of recycling odds and ends.

You will need:
- old Christmas cards
- children's scissors
- glitter or sequin's (optional)
- plain white postcards or cards made from plain pieces of card

The recipients of the cards will be equally thrilled with the thought.

1 Get your child to tidy up on Christmas morning and put their favourite bits and pieces starting with old Christmas cards, to one side for making the postcards.

2 Cut up and recycle these bits and pieces.

3 Use children's scissors to give decorative edges and, as Christmas is not quite over, you could add some glitter or sequins. Stick the bits onto plain white postcards or those you have made.

4 Write the thank you note on the back of the postcard, together with the address.

AG

WASSAIL (MULLED ALE)

Mulls were traditionally mixed at the fireside and heated with a red-hot poker. The wassail was a bowl from which health was drunk, especially on Christmas Eve and the Twelfth Night.

Serves 8 Preparation time: 15 minutes

4 small red apples
2¼ litres (4 pints) brown ale, e.g. Black Sheep
375 ml (½ bottle) sherry
½ teaspoon ground ginger
½ teaspoon ground nutmeg
1 cinnamon stick
2 strips of lemon rind
soft brown sugar, to taste
1 orange, cut into thin slices

1 Bake or microwave apples until just soft.

2 Put all the other ingredients into a large pan and bring slowly to the boil. Stir to dissolve the sugar.

3 Turn off the heat and leave to stand for a few minutes.

4 Strain into a warmed jug and serve in warm tankards, with a slice of orange on the top.

 Freezing not recommended

MEW

TROPICAL FRUIT PUNCH

This is a wonderfully refreshing non-alcoholic choice. You can keep the mixed fruit syrup in the refrigerator and make it up with the soda water or ginger beer as required. **Serves 8** Preparation time: 15 minutes + Cooling + Chilling

6 tablespoons granulated sugar

juice of 4 oranges

juice of 2 lemons

juice of 2 grapefruit

1 large mango, peeled and stone removed (or tinned)

1 litre (1¾ pints) soda water or traditional ginger beer

To serve

lemon or lime slices

mint leaves

1 Slowly bring the sugar and 6 tablespoons of water to boil in the saucepan. Allow this to simmer for 2 minutes to make a syrup. It will thicken slightly. Leave to cool.

2 Strain the fruit juices and mix them together in the jug.

3 Purée the mango using a liquidizer or mash the flesh with a fork and press it through a sieve. Stir the mango with the fruit juice and chill in the refrigerator.

4 When the syrup is cold, add it to the fruit juice mixture and chill in the refrigerator.

5 Add the chilled soda water or ginger beer and stir gently.

6 Serve the drink in long glasses with the lemon or lime slices and mint leaves.

 Freezing not recommended

MEW

CHRISTMAS EVE SUPPER FOR 8

Chicken Liver Pâté with Brandy and Garlic Mushrooms x 2 (page 104)

Rösti Topped Halibut with Smoked Salmon and Avocado x 2 (page 110)

Banoffee Tarts x 2 (page 114)

CHRISTMAS DAY LUNCH FOR 12

Spiced Cream of Watercress Soup with Cheesy Croutons x 2 (page 44)

Buttered Roast Turkey with Chestnut Stuffing (page 60)

Cranberry Kumquat Sauce (page 46)

Bacon and Chipolata Rolls x 2 (page 65)

Turkey Gravy x 2 (page 69)

Roast Potatoes x 2 (page 72)

Cheese Potato Bakes (page 77)

Creamed Brussels Sprouts with Chestnuts x 2 (page 74)

Baked Mustard and Orange Carrots x 2 (page 74)

Gran's Christmas Pudding (page 20)

Rum Sauce (page 22)

Christmas Ice Cream (page 53)

VEGETARIAN CHRISTMAS DAY FOR 6

Christmas Waldorf Salad with Grilled Goat's Cheese (page 70)

Mushroom Strudel (page 90)

Port Sauce (page 99)

Roast Potatoes (page 72)

Celeriac Purée with Fried Onions and Mustard Seeds (page 79)

Creamed Brussel Sprouts with Chestnuts (page 74)

Christmas Star Trifle (page 56)

BOXING DAY BRUNCH FOR 8

(on the assumption that people will have the same guests as on Christmas Eve!!)

Baked Brioche filled with Creamy Wild Mushrooms (page 124)

Kedgeree (page 123)

Muffin Toasties (page 132)

Leek and Sweet Potato Tortilla (page 133)

IMPROMPTU SUPPER FOR 6 INCLUDING 2 VEGETARIANS

Brie and Rocket Pasta Salad x 1 (page 138)

Turkey Stir-Fry (page 148)

Chestnut, Stilton and Spinach Stuffed Pancakes (page 142)

Mincemeat and Marzipan Ice Cream (page 152)

Christmas Fruit Compote (page 54)

BUFFET FOR 12 –18

Hummus and Red Pepper Crostini (page 164)

Goat's Cheese and Olive Crostini (page 164)

Salami and Sun-dried Tomato Boats (page 161)

Quails Eggs with Sea Salt and Chilli Dip (page 157)

Whole Poached Salmon (page 172)

Festive Eggs (page 174)

Green Mayonnaise Sauce (page 174)

Turkey Chilli (page 177)

Italian Plait (page 178)

Roasted Red Pepper and Tomato Sauce (page 87)

Sweet Pepper Pasta Salad (Tossed Green Salad) (page 183)

Stollen Bread and Butter Pudding (page 187)

Double Chocolate Clementine Cheesecake (page 188)

Raspberry Mousse Pavlova Gâteau (page 190)

DRINKS PARTY

Mulled Red Wine (page 199)

Spicy Fruit Cup (page 195)

Wassail (page 200)

Tiger Prawns with Chilli Mayonnaise (page 163)

Rarebit and Mango Toasts (page 162)

Ratatouille Croustades (page 158)

Mushroom Croustades (page 159)

Melon with Prosciutto Ham (page 166)

Mini Croissants (page 166)

Leek and Stilton Crackers (page 168)

Cherry Tomatoes with a Sardine Filling (page 157)

Mini Caramel and Chocolate Meringues (page 184)

Cherry and Chocolate Shortbread (page 185)

Mango Dates (page 185)

About the Women's Institute

The Women's Institute started in Britain in 1915 at Llanfairpwll PG, North Wales. During the First World War it was formed to encourage countrywomen to get involved in growing and preserving food to help to increase the supply of food to the war torn nation.

The WI has grown into the largest national charity for women with 220,000 members. Through close community ties and wide-ranging activities, the WI plays a unique role in enabling women to turn their interests into achievements and their concerns into campaigns.

The WI is an educational, social, non-party political and non-sectarian organisation, offering women the opportunity of learning, campaigning, friendship and sharing - not just in traditional interests such as arts and crafts but also in the latest developments in IT, health and fitness and science.

WI has an unrivalled reputation as a voice of reason, integrity and intelligence on issues that matter to women and their communities. Debt relief, human rights, support for British agriculture, sustainable development and climate change are just some of the issues currently on the WI's campaigning agenda. The members democratically decide all campaigning issues.

If you would like to know more about any aspect of the NFWI please contact:
National Federation of Women's Institutes
104 New Kings Road, London, SW6 4LY
tel: 020 7371 9300 – fax 020 7736 3652
e-mail hq@nfwi.org.uk – website www.women'sinstitute.org.uk

Recipe Index

The page numbers shown in **bold** *are illustrations.*

Ale, Mulled [Wassail], 200
Apples
    Apple, Mincemeat and Almond
        Crumble, 113
    Stuffed Apples, 58, 69
Apricots in Brandy, **144**, 146, **146**
Aromatic Pilaff Rice, **181**, 182
Asparagus, 138, **139**
Avocados, 106

Bacon and Chipolata Rolls, 65
Baked Brioches Filled with Creamy Wild
    Mushrooms, **125**, 124
Baked Mustard and Orange Carrots, **73**, **74**,
    74–75
Banana Smoothie, 196, **197**
Banoffee Tarts, 114, **115**
Beef in Beer with Prunes, 112
Biscuits
    Cherry and White Chocolate
        Shortbread, 185
    Christmas Cinnamon Stars, 34
    Florentines, **80**, 81
    Gingerbread Men, **32**, 33
    Scottish Shortbread, 30
    Special Millionaire Chocolate
        Squares, 31
Black Forest and White Chocolate Cheese
    Ring, 189
Boned Turkey Roll with Date, Orange and
    Almond Stuffing, 61
Braised Red Cabbage with Apple, 78–79
Brandy Butter, 22
Bread Sauce, 46, **47**
Breads
    Baked Brioches Filled with Creamy
        Wild Mushrooms, **120**, 126
    Christmas Stollen, 28, **29**
    Goat's Cheese and Olive Crostini,
        164–165
    Hummus and Red Pepper Crostini, 164
    Mini Croissants, 166, **167**
    Muffin Toasties, 132
    Mushroom Croustades, 159
    Rarebit and Mango Toasts, 162
    Ratatouille Croustades, 158
    Stollen Bread and Butter Pudding, 187
Breton Style Chicken Suprême with
    Calvados, 64
Brie, Asparagus and Rocket Pasta Salad,
    138, **139**

Broccoli and Stilton Roulade, **84**, 95
Brunches, 121–134
Bubble and Squeak Gratin, 142
Buttered Roast Turkey with Chestnut
    Stuffing, 60

Cabbage
    Braised Red Cabbage with Apple,
        78–79
    Bubble and Squeak Gratin, 142
Cakes
    Chocolate Christmas Cake, 18
    Chocolate Log, 52
    Christmas Cake, 12
    Italian Gâteau, 92, **93**
    Jewelled Christmas Cake, **10**, 15, **15**
    Raspberry Mousse Pavlova Gâteau,
        190–191
Caramelised Tropical Fruit Brochettes, **102**,
    118
Carrots
    Baked Mustard and Orange Carrots,
        73, **74**, 74–75
    Triple Vegetable Terrine, 136–137
Casseroles
    Oriental Ham, 150
    Turkey Chilli, 177
Celeriac
    Purée with Onions and Mustard Seeds,
        79
    Triple Vegetable Terrine, 136–137
Cheese dishes
    Brie, Asparagus and Rocket Pasta Salad,
        138, **139**
    Broccoli and Stilton Roulade, **84**, 95
    Bubble and Squeak Gratin, 142
    Cheesy Potato Bakes, 77
    Chestnut, Stilton and Spinach Stuffed
        Pancakes, 142–143
    Goat's Cheese and Olive Crostini,
        164–165
    Gruyère Cheese Puffs, 171
    Leek and Stilton Crackers, **167**, 168
    Party Peanut Butter and Cheese Whirls,
        170
    Potted Blue Cheese with Walnuts, 136
    Red Pepper Cheese Soufflés, 140, **141**
    Scrambled Eggs with Roquefort, 122
    Spinach and Boursin Pouches, 169
    Stilton and Walnut Mousses, 175
    Stuffed Mushroom and Caerphilly Tart,
        96, **97**
    Winter Vegetable and Caerphilly
        Crumble, 94
Cheesecakes, **154**, 188
Cherry and White Chocolate Shortbread,
    185

Cherry Tomatoes with a Sardine Filling, 157
Chestnut and Cranberry Stuffing Balls,
    88–89
Chestnut and Mushroom Roast, 86
Chestnut Stuffing, **47**, 48
Chestnut, Stilton and Spinach Stuffed
    Pancakes, 142–143
Chicken dishes
    Breton Style Chicken Suprême with
        Calvados, 64
    Chicken Liver Pâté with Brandy &
        Garlic Mushrooms, 104
Chilli
    Dip, 157
    Mayonnaise, 163
    Turkey, 177
Chocolate
    Black Forest and White Chocolate
        Cheese Ring, 189
    Cherry and White Chocolate
        Shortbread, 185
    Christmas Cake, 18
    Double Chocolate Clementine
        Cheesecake, **154**, 188
    Fudge, **50**, 51
    Iced Chocolate and Banana Smoothie,
        196, **197**
    Log, 52
    Mini Caramel and Chocolate
        Meringues, 184
    Orange Chocolate Truffles, 186
    Special Millionaire Chocolate Squares,
        31
Christmas
    Cake, 12
    Cider Punch, 195
    Cinnamon Stars, 34
    Fruit Compote, 54, **55**
    Ice Cream, 53
    Pudding, 19, 20, **21**, 151
    Star Trifle, **38**, 56, **56**
    Stollen, 28, **29**
    Waldorf Salad with Grilled Goat's
        Cheese, 70, **71**
Christmas Day timetable, 82–83
Cider punch, 195
Confectionery see Sweets
Couscous Salad with Harissa Dressing, 108,
    109
Cranberries
    Chestnut and Cranberry Stuffing Balls,
        88–89
    Cranberry and Port Sauce, 100
    Cranberry and apple Dressing, 175
    Cranberry Kumquat Sauce, 46, **47**
Creamed Brussels Sprouts with Chestnuts,
    73, 74, **74**

Croissants, Mini 166, **167**
Croutons, Cheesy, 44
Crumbles
    Apple, Mincemeat and Almond, 113
    Winter Vegetable and Stilton, 94
Cucumber and Dill Dressing, 42

Dates, Mango, 185
Desserts
    Apple, Mincemeat and Almond
      Crumble, 113
    Apricots in Brandy, **144**, 146, **146**
    Banoffee Tarts, 114, **115**
    Black Forest and White Chocolate
      Cheese Ring, 189
    Caramelised Tropical Fruit Brochettes,
      102, 118
    Chocolate Log, 52
    Christmas Fruit Compote, 54, **55**
    Christmas Ice Cream, 53
    Christmas Star Trifle, **38**, 56, **56**
    Double Chocolate Clementine
      Cheesecake, **154**, 188
    Fruity Christmas Pudding, 19
    Golden Meringue Queen of Christmas
      Puddings, 151
    Gran's Christmas Pudding, 20, **21**
    Mincemeat and Marzipan Ice Cream,
      134, 152, **152**
    Mini Caramel and Chocolate
      Meringues, 184
    Raspberry and Yogurt Crunch, 119
    Raspberry Mousse Pavlova Gâteau,
      190–191
    Stollen Bread and Butter Pudding, 187
see also Sweets
Dips
    Chilli, 157
    Chilli Mayonnaise, 163
Double Chocolate Clementine Cheesecake,
    154, 188
Double Decker Christmas Special
    Sandwich, 124, **125**
Dressings
    Cranberry, 175
    Cucumber and Dill, 42
    Harissa, 108, **109**
    Olive Oil with Chilli and Garlic, 147
Drinks, 194–201
    Alcoholic, **192**, 195, 199, 200
    Non-alcoholic, 195, 201
    Punches, 195
    Smoothies, 196, **197**

Eggs
    Festive Eggs, **173**, 174
    Muffin Toasties, 132

Quail's Eggs with Sea Salt and Chilli
    Dip, 157
Scrambled Eggs with Roquefort, 122

Festive Eggs, **173**, 174
Fish dishes
    Kedgeree, 123
    Prawns with Avocado and Fennel, 106,
      107
    Rösti-Topped Halibut with Smoked
      Salmon and Avocado, 110, **111**
    Sole, Prawn and Spinach Roulades, 66,
      67
    Tiger Prawns with Chilli Mayonnaise,
      163
    Whole Poached Salmon, 172, **173**
Florentines, **80**, 81
Fruit dishes
    Apricots in Brandy, **144**, 146, **146**
    Cakes, 12, 15, 18
    Caramelised Tropical Fruit Brochettes,
      102, 118
    Christmas Fruit Compote, 54, **55**
    Fruity Christmas Pudding, 19
    Fruity Pork with Ginger, 180, **181**
    Goat's Cheese and Olive Crostini,
      164
    Iced Chocolate and Banana Smoothie,
      196, **197**
    Mango Dates, 185
    Melon with Prosciutto Ham, 166, **167**
    Prawns with Avocado and Fennel, 106,
      107
    Rarebit and Mango Toasts, 162
    Raspberry and Yogurt Crunch, 119
    Raspberry Mousse Pavlova Gâteau,
      190–191
    Spicy Fruit Cup, 195
Fudge, **50**, 51

Garlic Mushrooms, 104
Ginger, Fruity Pork with, 180, **181**
Gingerbread Men, **32**, 33
Glamorgan Sausages, 88
Glühwein [Mulled Red Wine], **192**, 199
Goat's Cheese and Olive Crostini, 164
Golden Meringue Queen of Christmas
    Puddings, 151
Goose, Roasted with Thickened Gravy, **58**,
    62, 62–63
Gran's Christmas Pudding, 20, **21**
Gravy
    Onion, 128, **129**
    Thickened, 63
    Turkey, 69
    see also Sauces
Green Mayonnaise Sauce, 175

Gruyére Cheese Puffs, 171

Ham
    Honey and Fig Baked Ham, 40
    Melon with Prosciutto Ham, 166, **167**
    Oriental Ham Casserole, 150
Harissa Dressing, 108, **109**
Hollandaise Sauce, 66, **67**
Holly's Christmas Filo Pie, 98
Honey and Fig Baked Ham, 40
Hummus and Red Pepper Crostini, 164

Ice cream
    Christmas, 53
    Mincemeat and Marzipan, **134**, 152, **152**
Iced Chocolate and Banana Smoothie, 196,
    197
Icing, Royal, 14
Italian Gâteau, 92, **93**
Italian Plait, 178, **179**

Jewelled Christmas Cake, **10**, 15, **15**

Kedgeree, 123
Kumquats, 46, **47**

Leek and Stilton Crackers, **167**, 168
Leek and Sweet Potato Tortilla, 132–133

Mango Dates, 185
Marzipan, 13
Mincemeat and Marzipan Ice Cream, **134**,
    152, **152**
Mayonnaise
    Chilli, 163
    Green, 175
Melon with Prosciutto Ham, 166, **167**
Menu planning, 156, 202–203
Meringues, Mini Caramel and Chocolate,
    184
Mince pies, 24, **25**
Mincemeat, 26
    Apple, Mincemeat and Almond
      Crumble, 113
    Mincemeat and Marzipan Ice Cream,
      134, 152, **152**
Mini Caramel and Chocolate Meringues,
    184
Mini Croissants, 166, **167**
Mousses
    Black Forest and White Chocolate
      Cheese Ring, 189
    Raspberry Mousse Pavlova Gâteau,
      190–191
    Smoked Salmon and Garlic, 42, **43**
    Stilton and Walnut, 175

Muffin Toasties, 132
Mulled Red Wine [Glühwein], **192**, 199
Mushrooms
    Baked Brioches Filled with Creamy
        Wild Mushrooms, **125**, 124
    Chestnut and Mushroom Roast, 86
    Garlic, 104
    Mushroom Croustades, 159
    Mushroom Strudel, 90, **91**
    Stuffed Mushroom and Stilton Tart, 96,
        97
    Warm Mushroom and Spinach, 131
    Wild Mushroom and Artichoke Pie,
        105
    Wild Mushroom Pâté, 89
Mustard Mash, 130–131

Olive Oil with Chilli and Garlic, 147
Orange Chocolate Truffles, 186
Oriental Ham Casserole, 150

Pancakes, 142–143
Parsnip Dauphinoise, **73**, 75, **75**
Party food, 155–191
Party Peanut Butter and Cheese Whirls, 170
Pasta
Brie, Asparagus and Rocket Pasta Salad,
    138, **139**
Sweet Pepper Pasta Salad, 183
Pastry dishes
    Banoffee Tarts, 114, **115**
    Gruyère Cheese Puffs, 171
    Italian Plait, 178, **179**
    Leek and Stilton Crackers, **167**, 168
    Mushroom Strudel, 90, **91**
    Party Peanut Butter and Cheese Whirls,
        170
    Star Mince Pies, 24, **25**
    Stuffed Mushroom and Stilton Tart, 96,
        97
    see also Pies
Pâtés
    Chicken Liver, 104
    Wild Mushroom, 89
Pavlova, Raspberry Mousse Gateau,
    190–191
Peppers
    Hummus and Red Pepper Crostini, 164
    Red Pepper Cheese Soufflés, 140, **141**
    Roasted Red Pepper and Tomato Sauce,
        87
    Sweet Pepper Pasta Salad, 183
Pies
    Holly's Christmas Filo, 98
    Wild Mushroom and Artichoke, 105
    see also Pastry dishes
Pork dishes

Fruity Pork with Ginger, 180, **181**
Pork Sausages with Caramelised Onion
    Gravy, 128, **129**
Port Sauce, 99
Potatoes
    Bubble and Squeak Gratin, 142
    Cheesy Potato Bakes, 77
    Leek and Potato Tortilla, 132–133
    Mustard Mash, 130–131
    Roast potatoes, 72, **73**
Potted Blue Cheese with Walnuts, 136
Poultry dishes
    Boned Turkey Roll, 61
    Breton Style Chicken Suprême with
        Calvados, 64
    Buttered Roast Turkey, 60
    Chicken Liver Pâté, 104
    Roast Goose with Thickened Gravy, **58**,
        62, 62–63
    Turkey Chilli, 177
    Turkey Stir-Fry, 148, **149**
Prawns
Sole, Prawn and Spinach Roulades, 66, **67**
Tiger Prawns with Chilli Mayonnaise, 163
with Avocado and Fennel, 106, **107**
Puddings *see* Desserts
Punches *see* Drinks

Quail's Eggs with Sea Salt and Chilli Dip,
    157

Rarebit and Mango Toasts, 162
Raspberry and Yogurt Crunch, 119
Raspberry Mousse Pavlova Gâteau,
    190–191
Ratatouille Croustades, 158
Red Pepper Cheese Soufflés, 140, **141**
Rice, Aromatic Pilaff, **181**, 182
Roast Goose with Thickened Gravy, **58**, **62**,
    62–63
Roast Potatoes, 72, **73**
Roasted Red Pepper and Tomato Sauce, 87
Rösti-Topped Halibut with Smoked Salmon
    and Avocado, 110, **111**
Roulades
    Broccoli and Stilton, **84**, 95
    Sole, Prawn and Spinach, 66, **67**
Royal Icing, 14
Rum Sauce, 22

Sage, Onion and Pickled Walnut Stuffing,
    47, 49
Salads
    Brie, Asparagus and Rocket Pasta Salad,
        138, **139**
    Christmas Waldorf Salad with Grilled
        Goat's Cheese, 70, **71**

Couscous Salad with Harissa Dressing,
    108, **109**
Sweet Pepper Pasta, 183
Warm Mushroom and Spinach, 131
Salami and Sun-Dried Tomato Boats, 161
Salmon
    Muffin Toasties, 132
    Rösti-Topped Halibut with Smoked
        Salmon & Avocado, 110, **111**
    Smoked Salmon and Garlic Mousse,
        42, **43**
    Whole Poached Salmon, 172, **173**
Sandwiches, 124, **125**
Sauces
    Bread, 46, **47**
    Cranberry and Port, 100
    Cranberry Kumquat, 46, **47**
    Green Mayonnaise, 175
    Hollandaise, 66, **67**
    Port, 99
    Rum, 22
    Sun-Dried Tomato, 100
    Tomato Sauce, 87
    see also Gravy
Sausages
Bacon and Chipolata Rolls, 65
Glamorgan Sausages, 88
Pork Sausages with Caramelised Onion
    Gravy, 128, **129**
Salami and Sun-Dried Tomato Boats, 161
Vegetarian, 88
Scottish Shortbread, 30
Scrambled Eggs with Roquefort, 122
Shortbreads, 30, 31, 185
Smoked Salmon and Garlic Mousse, 42, **43**
Smoothies *see* Drinks
Snacks
    Double Decker Christmas Special
        Sandwich, 124, **125**
    Muffin Toasties, 132
Sole, Prawn and Spinach Roulades with
    Hollandaise Sauce, 66, **67**
Soufflé, Red Pepper Cheese, 140, **141**
Soup, Spiced Cream of Watercress, 44, **45**
Special Millionaire Chocolate Squares, 31
Spiced Cream of Watercress Soup, 44, **45**
Spicy Fruit Cup, 195
Spinach
    Spinach and Boursin Pouches, 169
    Warm Mushroom and Spinach Salad,
        131
Sprouts
    Bubble and Squeak Gratin, 142
    Creamed Brussels Sprouts with
        Chestnuts, **73**, 74, **74**
    Triple Vegetable Terrine, 136–137
Star Mince Pies, 24, **25**

Starters
Baked Brioches Filled with Creamy
Wild Mushrooms, **125**, 124
Broccoli and Stilton Roulade, **84**, 95
Couscous Salad with Harissa Dressing,
108, **109**
Prawns with Avocado and Fennel, 106,
107
Red Pepper Cheese Soufflés, 140, **141**
Stilton and Walnut Mousses, 175
Stir-fry, Turkey, 148, **149**
Stollen Bread and Butter Pudding, 187
Stollen, 28, **29**
Strudel, Mushroom, 90, **91**
Stuffed Apples, **58**, 69
Stuffed Mushroom and Stilton Tart, 96, **97**
Stuffings
Chestnut, **47**, 48
Chestnut and Cranberry Stuffing Balls,
88–89
Chestnut, Stilton and Spinach, 142–143
Sage, Onion and Pickled Walnut, **47**, 49
Sun-Dried Tomato Sauce, 100
Sweet Pepper Pasta Salad, 183
Sweets
Chocolate Fudge, **50**, 51
Orange Chocolate Truffles, 186
see also Desserts

Tarts *see* Pastry dishes
Terrine, Triple Vegetable, 136–137
Tiger Prawns with Chilli Mayonnaise, 163
Timetable, Christmas Day, 82–83
Tomatoes
Cherry Tomatoes with a Sardine Filling,
157
Salami and Sun-Dried Tomato Boats, 161
Sun-Dried Tomato Sauce, 100
Tortillas, 132–133
Trifle, Christmas Star, **38**, 56, **56**
Triple Vegetable Terrine, 136–137
Tropical Fruit Punch, 201
Truffles, Orange Chocolate, 186
Turkey
Boned Turkey Roll, 61
Buttered Roast Turkey, 60
Chilli, 177
Double Decker Christmas Special
Sandwich, 124, **125**
Gravy, 69
Stir-Fry, 148, **149**

Vegetable dishes
Baked Mustard and Orange Carrots,
73, **74**, 74–75
Braised Red Cabbage with Apple, 78–79

Broccoli and Stilton Roulade, **84**, 95
Bubble and Squeak Gratin, 142
Celeriac Purée with Onions and
Mustard Seeds, 79
Cheesy Potato Bakes, 77
Chestnut and Mushroom Roast, 86
Chestnut, Stilton and Spinach Stuffed
Pancakes, 142–143
Creamed Brussels Sprouts with
Chestnuts, **73**, 74, **74**
Garlic Mushrooms, 104
Holly's Christmas Filo Pie, 98
Italian Plait, 178, **179**
Leek and Potato Tortilla, 132–133
Leek and Stilton Crackers, **167**, 168
Mushroom Strudel, 90, **91**
Mustard Mash, 130–131
Parsnip Dauphinoise, **73**, 75, **75**
Ratatouille Croustades, 158
Red Pepper Cheese Soufflés, 140, **141**
Roast Potatoes, 72, **73**
Roasted Red Pepper and Tomato Sauce,
87
Salami and Sun-Dried Tomato Boats, 161
Stuffed Mushroom and Stilton Tart, 96,
97
Triple Vegetable Terrine, 136–137
Wild Mushroom and Artichoke Pie, 105
Wild Mushroom Pâté, 89
Winter Vegetable and Caerphilly
Crumble, 94
Vegetarian dishes, 85–93

Waldorf Salad, 70, **71**
Warm Mushroom and Spinach Salad, 131
Wassail [Mulled Ale], 200
Welsh Rarebit, 162
Whole Poached Salmon, 172, **173**
Wild Mushroom and Artichoke Pie, 105
Wild Mushroom Pâté, 89
Wine, Mulled Red [Glühwein], **192**, 199
Winter Vegetable and Caerphilly Crumble, 94

Yogurt Crunch, Raspberry, 119

Craft Index

Aromatherapy bags, **57**, 57
see also gift bags; organza bags

baskets, fabric, 101
beaded wire stars, **16**, 17
bottles, shirt-tie wrap for, 176
bows, 78

candles, 26, 194
cardholders, 99
Christmas cards, 23
see also thank you cards
Christmas hampers, 41
cord, **36**, 37
crackers, alternative, **76**, 77

food hampers, 41

games, 165
garlands, 65
gift bags, 153
see also aromatherapy bags; organza
bags
gift tags, 130
glass balls, 127
glass jars and bottles, decorated, **144**, 145

hampers, 41

ivy, 122

jars and bottles, decorated, **144**, 145

mirror balls, **160**, 161
mistletoe balls, 113

notebooks, handmade, 68, **68**

organza bags, **50**, 51
see also aromatherapy bags; gift bags

pine cones, 133
place names, 87
pomanders, **198**, 199

ribbons, **36**, 37, 78

snow globes, 191
snowflakes, decorative, **16**, 17
snowmen, soap powder, 143
soaps, as gifts, 137
stars, beaded wire, 16, 17
stationery, 68, **68**, 200

table decorations, 87, 122, 194
alternative crackers, **76**, 77
candles, 26, 194
wreaths, **116**, 117
tassels, 27
thank you cards, 200
see also Christmas cards

wrapping gifts, 35, **35**, **36**, 37
wreaths, **116**, 117